Osborn
on
Osborn

Osborn on Osborn

ROBERT OSBORN

New Haven and New York · Ticknor & Fields · 1982

Designed by Murray Belsky

Printed in the United States of America

H 10 9 8 7 6 5 4 3 2 1

Library of Congress Cataloging in Publication Data

Osborn, Robert Chesley, 1904–
    Osborn on Osborn.

    1. Osborn, Robert Chesley, 1904–   . 2. Cartoonists
—United States—Biography. I. Title.
NC1429.062A2 1982   741.5′092′4 [B]   81-18492
ISBN 0-89919-051-0   AACR2

To Nicolas and Eliot Osborn, Mary Barnes, the Lionnis, the Breuers, Miss Boucher, Miss Marvin, Uncle Samuel, who survived Libby Prison, Kate Osborn, the Motherwells, Orlēna, the various Hills, Fred Hartman, Amanda Rasmussen, Witherspoon and John Gee at Yale, Wilder Hobson, Wynkoop as well. Fry, Bell, Ralph Barton, Palmer Cox, the Lynes, surely Nancy Wilson Ross, the Calders, ELODIE. Doctors Wieler, O'Connell, Wylie, Ferguson, and Sippy. Ophélia de Rougé, the Will Burtins, Curt Valentin, Mike Straight, G. Harrison, Jung, Ed Thompson, Elizabeth Hardwick, Keaton, Chaplin and Fields, Griswold and Brewster, the Wolkonskys, Mima Mellon, Sandra, the Wohls, Edith Halpert, the Mumfords, Pete Scoville, Freud, and to all who work against the relentless PROMISE of KILLING, and FOR the *joys* of life. The list is endless, and is given in gratitude.

—R.O.

FOREWORD by Garry Trudeau

In modern times, there have been a few important American artists—Robert Osborn, Saul Steinberg, and David Levine come to mind—who have indulged themselves a promiscuous interest in cartooning, only to wake one day and find to their horror that they were widely regarded as cartoonists. Since more often than not the cartoons paid the rent, there was precious little they could do about it, save possibly calling their galleries to satisfy themselves that they were still being taken seriously in noncartooning circles.

Bob Osborn doesn't have much to say about being a cartoonist in this book, perhaps because by choosing to call himself a "drawer," he lets us make up our own minds as to the genus of his genius. This is mischievous of him, but not entirely unexpected. After all, by his own admission he has always been preoccupied with how things *felt*, not how they looked. Still, since he refuses to flag us down at any convenient signpost, we are free to draw our own parochial conclusions, and mine is that Robert Osborn is one of the very few true masters of illustrative cartooning.

This was not always apparent. Early on, Osborn passed up all opportunities for cheap, overnight success, preferring instead to hone his skills, pad his portfolio, and live in quiet squalor in the bowels of Paris. His early work, he claims, was hopelessly derivative, but so is *all* early work, and what better place to marinate in the great painting traditions than Paris in the twenties? To aficionados of the period, Osborn's youth must seem endlessly serendipitous, especially given the artist's uncanny knack for chance encounters, à la *Ragtime*, with notables of the day. One day, he bumps into Picasso buying forty tubes of zinc white at a Parisian art store. On another occasion, he meets the great Brancusi, who dispenses epigrams from the edge of his bathtub. W. H. Auden regales him with an homage to Freud at a seaside resort in Portugal. He is sent by a local newspaper to draw actress Katharine Cornell in her hotel suite, and, infatuated in the extreme, returns with 108 drawings. Such was the happy education of R. Osborn.

Character-building, though, comes only with adversity, and it was the chastened, post-Munich Osborn who finally found his stride and his first audience. The latter was comprised largely of Navy airmen, who delighted in the antics of Cadet Pilot Dilbert, cartoon star of a series of training manuals that Osborn illustrated while stationed in Washington. This was back when the Pentagon still entertained simple solutions to big problems, and the big problem they handed Osborn was how to keep pilots from killing themselves before the enemy did. Osborn's simple solution was irreverent humor and a clean line, and it set him on a course for life. Propelled by a deeply moral sensibility, Osborn thereafter used his pen to sort out the good from the bad in an era that abounded with both. Celebratory of its heroes and unsparing of its rogues, Osborn drew the world as it felt to him, and the world cheered him on. In the heyday of magazine and book illustration, no finer interpreter of mores and manners, no deadlier exposer of chicanery and foolishness, no happier chronicler of genius and grace, was working in American graphic arts. Today Osborn is as astute and prolific as ever, but the outlets are fewer, and his admirers are famished. We are thus deeply indebted to his publisher for the feast herein.

Robert Osborn
drawing in the
studio after

I draw what I feel, it is as simple as that, and the stronger the feeling the better the picture. The drawings I like best seem to come right out of my unconscious—fullblown and no changes made—and they are, of course, what I am.

This is probably the problem—to discover who you are; to end up being one person; to be clear and aware of who you are and what you believe in.

SLOW LEARNER

I was born.

Actually in Oshkosh, Wisconsin, on October 26, 1904, at 2:00 A.M. in my parents' bedroom. A peppery Dr. Clarke delivered me. He and Mrs. Clarke were good friends of the family.

I was a very slow, very naive learner, thank heaven.

For a long time I assumed that Dr. Clarke had brought me like some package to 756 Algoma Street in his deep maroon car, which passengers entered by a rear step and door, and that he had come up our cement sidewalk, rung the bell, and handed me to one of the housemaids.

Also, I really believed in Santa Claus until I was at least ten. After all, I had actually seen him, at six-thirty one Christmas morning, from beneath a pull-down green shade. He was not large, was vermilion-clad, a fat little man moving swiftly about the next-door neighbors' living room, depositing presents here and there beneath the Radfords' balsam tree. The whole act was suddenly over and he was gone. I was instantly afraid that he had seen me and would pass our chimney by as he circled the earth.

R. O., 1907

My long-lived faith in Santa was certainly reinforced by that neighbor, Mr. Radford of the Radford Lumber Company—a totally impractical man. He started twenty-four different businesses; all of them failed. He used his wife's dowry until it had vanished. He raised pure white collies, his specialty, and even gave one to Calvin Coolidge. He imported Dutch bulbs by the thousands, all of which perished from lack of care.

But it was he who bothered to send to his two daughters, Phyllis and Molly; and to Chandler, my older brother, four years my senior; and to me . . . don't forget me! . . . letters clearly postmarked "The North Pole," saying in a trembly hand that he "had indeed received our Christmas lists" (which the four of us had ceremoniously sent up the chimney in our living room, flinging them into the flames, which whipped them away magically intact), and that he would "try to attend to our desires."

The first crack in this yearly Christmas idyll occurred when, after a fullblown reply from Santa Claus, I found *my* letter, slightly singed, on the side lawn.

My belief was soon restored by a careful reading of my treasured 1908 volume of *Tommy Trot's Visit to Santa Claus* by Thomas Nelson Page, with superb oil-painting illustrations by Victor C. Anderson.

However, the final blow came one summer afternoon when Molly Radford told me in no uncertain terms that *there was no Santa Claus,* that all the other children knew it, and that it was just our mothers and fathers who made it happen. She was, I am sure, trying to do me a kindness, but as that whole world dissolved before my eyes, I cried.

Santa Claus

PARENTS

Alice Lydia Wyckoff, my mother, was born in Detroit on June 30, 1873. Her father worked for the *Detroit Free Press*. He was a philanderer, which was hard on Alice's very decent, beautiful mother.

There was a sister, Jessie, and two brothers, Fred and Homer. Fred became a missionary in darkest Africa where his first wife, a Canadian, died of dengue fever. Later, he remarried, worked for the Ford Motor Company, and took to playing bridge and drinking martinis. Homer, an electrical engineer, was the inventor of a copper device to switch phone-call connections. His patent was infringed upon by rascals who copied the idea, did it in another metal, and could not be prosecuted for their cheating. He had an artistic flair, was obviously sensitive, drew well, and designed posters for his Presbyterian church.

My mother's family all lived in the old Governor Cass residence at 50 Perry Street. We used to be taken there by train to visit when I was ten or so. I hated it, and disliked Uncle Fred with his long neck and constant snuffling. Then, too, there were three older boys across the street who said that they were going to kill me. They showed me a revolver that was no toy. I stayed indoors at 50 Perry and drew endlessly for two weeks. I was scared and miserable.

My mother had gumption. She also had musical ability. She studied the piano, played very well, and with enjoyment. After graduating from the Detroit School of Music at nineteen, she got a job teaching music in three grade schools, all of which were in the vicinity of Ironwood, Michigan, a lumber and iron ore town in the upper peninsula. Across the river, tough Hurley, Wisconsin, boasted a main street with three solid blocks of saloons. On a small hill just outside the town stood the stockade in which the prostitutes were kept like so many prisoners.

Mother lived with the Luther Wrights. He was the

Alice

superintendent of a Michigan state prison. Very grim. Some years later I met him at their summer camp on Lake Gogebic. One afternoon my parents and the Wrights were playing whist on the open veranda and I was being a noisy nuisance. Suddenly Luther Wright glared at me and said, "Do you know what we do to prisoners? We strip them, wrap them in canvas soaked in salt water, and beat them with leather straps. I'll do that to you." I vanished, and loathed him from then on.

Mrs. Wright, on the contrary, couldn't have been nicer—a very jolly woman, always adding to the fun. It was she who took my mother into their Ironwood household, gave her a large sunlit room, and generally protected her. It was at their house that Alice met my father, an energetic young lumberman fifteen years her senior.

Each day, Alice would have breakfast at seven, then, rain or shine, she would set off to walk ten miles a day between three schools, to teach singing and harmony for one hour at each. On some winter days in that northern country the temperature would get down to thirty degrees below zero. No one ever spoke of windchill factors.

I can imagine how charming and sprightly she must have been, her cheeks aglow, her nutria muff held to her mouth. She was very pretty, had a personal style of which she was almost unwitting, and an exuberance that remained undaunted until two days before her death at eighty-two.

Even in her eighties she walked a mile a day and puttered in her small garden. After a stroke, which was to end her life within six weeks, I went to see her in the hospital. The left side of her face was already motionless and sagging. As I came in, she remarked, "I certainly look funny, don't I?" She was plucky, considerate, and sensitive and, all told, a remarkable woman to have known.

My father, Albert, was an early-on Wisconsin lumberman. Edna Ferber wrote about him and his friends in *Come and Get It* as "lumber barons," which he clearly was not.

He was born in Iola, Wisconsin, September 9, 1858, and he died in the Mayo Clinic on April 19, 1940, of a totally engulfing cancer, at age eighty-two.

Four years after Albert was born, his mother died. He once said to me, "Had she lived, I think that I would have

Father and his brother

been quite a different person."

His father was a judge in Oshkosh. Two years after my grandmother died, the judge married a cold ramrod of a woman, clothed always in black bombazine, who told the infatuated judge that she could not stand children and that Albert would have to be sent elsewhere. Father and his younger brother, Arthur, were thus banished from the judge's house and sent to live on a farm outside Waupaca, Wisconsin. There they were brought up by Uncle Samuel, who was tall, lithe, and a great rifle shot. As a boy of thirteen Samuel had gone off to the Civil War as a drummer in the Union Army. He was captured, and nearly died in Libby Prison. He was a kindly man. His wife, Della, ugly as sin but also kind, took my father in until, at sixteen, he was old enough to return to Oshkosh, where he taught at a one-room school.

Father and his brother became lumbermen when they bought one acre of timber in northern Wisconsin, bordering the narrow Wisconsin River. The first winter the two of them, aged seventeen and eighteen, lived in a canvas tent and, with a long two-handled saw, cut down all of their trees, bound them together into a raft, and rode it down the Wisconsin, into the Mississippi, and on to St. Louis. They sold their logs there. With their money, the brothers returned to northern Wisconsin, bought three more acres, and the next winter they sawed those trees, barged them south again, sold the logs, and returned north. They then bought eight acres and started hiring woodsmen to cut and barge the logs south each spring. Father finally acquired and ran three lumber companies and two land-buying companies. No wonder the money poured in.

The lumberjacks father hired to saw in the northern woods of Wisconsin and Michigan between 1885 and 1910 did incredible, often dangerous jobs. They did them well, and knew that they did them well. They took great pride in the number of trees they could fell in a day with their long two-handled saws. Father told of one man who, with his partner, would cut sixty-five large trees (and by large I mean three to four feet on the stump), day after day, with only Sundays off, all winter long. The cutting went on until the snow had melted and the logs could no longer be sledded for the spring drive to a saw-

Father's stepmother

15

Load of logs

The Tiffany lamp

mill, where they arrived either by river or on a very primitive railroad that had been laid out in the forests.

Today, of course, it crosses my mind that there were really no restrictions of any kind on men like my father and all of his friends. They literally could do anything to advance their enterprises. "Laissez-faire" is a weak word for it. They could cut hundreds of acres of timber without reforesting them, and they took no responsibility for the labor they hired at the going price. Health, welfare, retirement benefits? Unheard of! Cutthroat competition was the rule, and unless you stole you were free to do exactly as you wished. In the process they did produce a great deal of the lumber needed by the homesteaders moving westward.

In the end, these freewheeling activities were cut down to a socially acceptable level. Senator Robert La Follette finally forced reforestation upon the lumber industry and instigated the clearing up of "slashings" left on the ground. (Father loathed him, mainly because he felt that he was intellectually dishonest and a demagogue.)

When the family gathered for dinner when Chandler and I were young, father would pronounce judgment on anything which seemed wrong to him, and he would state, "I don't care if everyone in this city believes one way and I believe the other, I will stand for what I believe in!" Then he would unabashedly smite the round mahogany table with its gross, curved legs, causing the Tiffany lamp above to quaver and shake until the scared serving maid would fall back into the pantry through its squeaky swinging door.

But to us, father was kindly, honest, and truly just in all things. This balance was easy to live with as a child. We knew exactly where we floated in relation to the adult world. He was firm, yes, but never overly demanding (though at certain ages Chandler and I probably thought so). The main virtue of this man was the sense of his resolved manliness, which we felt unconsciously when we were young but which persists to this day when he occasionally appears in my dreams. I am always surprised and pleased to see him there, slightly removed from the scene but exactly as I remember him, even to the expensive but crumpled suits.

When Pavlova danced in the Oshkosh Opera House, with its white and gold interior, father was so moved by the *Dying Swan* that he (and many others of that staid and correct lot of lumbermen) stood on the scarlet velvet seats applauding and shouting and finally waving their breast-pocket handkerchiefs. As mother tugged at his coattails to pull father back down, I looked up at him to see tears of joy streaming down his cheeks. Never before had I seen in him such a marvelous outpouring of emotion.

At the end of his life he wrote to me from the Mayo Clinic, after the preliminary diagnosis but before the surgery for his fatal cancer. His words conveyed the character of the man. I see few like him today.

"I do not feel blue or discouraged," he wrote. "If my time has come, well and good. I have lived a long time, most of it triumphantly. There is a lot I would like to do but it may go undone. How blessed it is to have had Mother and Chandler and you."

Pavlova

Albert in duck blind at eighty

THE HOUSE

After mother and father were married in Ironwood, and Chandler had been born in Hurley, the family moved to Oshkosh because the schools were better. That sawmill town was laid out along an Algoma Indian trail, curves and all, on the northern side of the wonderful Fox River. Father was making so much money at the time from his sawmills in Michigan and Wisconsin that, as he once told me, "I didn't know how I would be able to spend it." The Depression took care of that problem in 1929!

Our house was an egregious combination of mechanically chipped stonework that failed to blend with dark brown shingles, screen porches, high-peaked roofs, tall chimneys, striped awnings, and heavy "Romanesque" (à la Sullivan) arches. The living room was two stories high, with a barrel vault and a strange oriental lamp made of brass, which cast down a very mysterious light upon the Steinway concert grand—beside which

756 Algoma Street

hung a large sepia reproduction of one of those Ville d'Avray Corots.

In all, our house had thirty-two rooms if one counted large storage spaces. Now, when I wish to get back to sleep, I try in my mind to place each room, starting with the basement and its monster boiler above the wood furnace, then the root cellar, then the billiard room, the wine cellar, and so on up to the large attic, with its water tank up a fifth flight of small stairs and most of its spaces, except the hunting room and the cook's small bedroom and toilet, not plastered but simply covered with pine-slat walls. I carefully place and orient the spaces, the wood used, the sounds, echoes, and odors.

The barn was large and roomy, with two horse stalls, a tack room, and a smaller space for the cow. The chickens lived at the rear. There was also an ice house which would be filled each winter with large cakes of ice cut from the frozen Fox River three blocks south of the house.

After I was delivered to that house, Chandler and I began the pure bliss of childhood. But first I had to survive a devastating early period of undernourishment which was so bad that they had to call in a specialist from Milwaukee, who came with a plump Irish nurse named Miss McGovern, to save me. Miss McGovern stayed on and became part of my life through World War I. Large and strong Amanda Rasmussen, the Danish cook who was with us for sixteen years, also became part of our lives, as did wiry Fred Hartman, the German gardener and handyman. These three had a strong effect upon me as a child.

Fred Hartman was generally a true Christian soul. The one momentary flaw was when the Kaiser's German armies were chewing up the French and English armies in 1914 and even I, quite young, noticed that Fred was so proud of Germany's fighting ability that he stamped his foot and slapped his knee just as Hitler was to do later in the Compiègne forest after swiftly defeating the French.

If Fred failed his Christian principles with that one revealing atavistic act, the citizens of Oshkosh failed him often and openly during that war. They literally spat on his face. He would tell me of these confrontations once he got back to our house, the sputum darkening wet on his

An emaciated child

grey coat, a terrible anger in his eyes.

It is good to remember that Fred, who couldn't write his name in English and was always compelled to sign an X for it, raised, with his hard-working wife, three sons who prospered later in their own lumberyards, and a daughter who graduated Phi Beta Kappa from the University of Wisconsin and remained there to become a professor of Advanced German.

As a young girl, Amanda Rasmussen had tended geese all day in Denmark. Oshkosh relatives vouched for her character and paid for her passage to America. She came to our household, where mother taught her English and where she became the cook to pale many cooks. Two of mother's "friends" were sneaky enough to try to hire her away, which caused real flames to shoot out of mother's ears for two whole days.

Amanda returned to Denmark to marry a decent Dane and had three sons. One, touchingly named Robert, runs a large and lively bookstore in Copenhagen. Amanda and I wrote one another perhaps once or twice a year, and certainly at Christmastime, until she died. I believe that toward the end of her life she knew how strong and worthy a person she was.

Fred and Amanda

IMAGINATION

It was my mother who really nurtured my imagination—not too consciously, but she did. It was she who brought back from Milwaukee or Chicago the Palmer Cox "Brownies" books; then the Arthur Rackham illustrations; and Kenneth Grahame's *The Wind in the Willows*, illustrated by Paul Branson; and Peter Newell's wild and delightful *The Hole Book*, with a quarter-inch hole punched clean through the book after Tom Potts unexpectedly fires a revolver on page one; and *The Slant Book*, which was actually cut in a rhomboid shape so that a youngster in a baby carriage—once free of his nurse's grasp—goes coasting down one page after another, snapping hydrants, sailing through bass drums, and tearing down tennis nets, until he finally plows into a haystack.

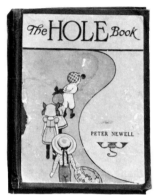
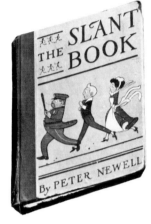
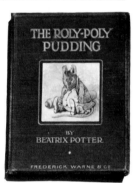

It is the parents' respect for and enjoyment of the endless world of the imagination that saves it for the child. Most children, at far too early an age, are already sodden-headed from being ordered, all along the line, to fit in, be like the others, grow up, stop fantasizing. The pretend worlds don't pay. It's the *real* stuff that counts!

To all this I say, "Rubbish!" and urge parents not to belittle in any way the feelings of their all-too-plodding offspring. Back their luminous ids, their strange imaginings, whether you understand them or not, for they will all too soon be cut down. A case in point: the capacity in *every* child to draw clearly and with a sense of color and tone is too often stolen by the adults who blindly say, "All tree trunks are black, all leaves are green." Or, "Today we will give you tracings of Santa to color RED!"

Mother always read to us before bedtime or when we were sick—Lewis Carroll, James Barrie, Kate Greenaway, and all of Beatrix Potter. Too, there was a magazine called *St. Nicholas* that arrived each month full of stories, pictures, and contests. Chandler and I submitted any number of drawings and photographs until each of us had won honorable mentions, then silver medals, and finally, gold medals.

All of these things inflamed our imaginations. I weep for today's children with their monotonous, crass, and manipulated TV fare.

There was one picture, illustrating John Ruskin's *The King of the Golden River*, that scared me. The first time mother turned the page exposing it I was petrified. It was a horrid, dark picture of a sinister dwarf knocking on a rain-swept front door. A frightened young girl, having flung open the window, stares down at him. The dwarf's nose seems to be covered by a fold of skin from his cheeks. It repelled me and fascinated me. Later, standing before the glass-doored book cabinet in the upper hall, I would steel myself, pull out the leather-bound book, turn to the exact page and give it an oblique glance. It still makes me uneasy, even at seventy-six.

GROWING UP IN OSHKOSH

The two Radford daughters next door, just across the driveway's turnaround with its fancy red canna bed, were almost exactly Chandler's and my ages. Phyllis, the older girl, defended me in any confrontation, and Chandler defended Molly. One tends to forget such alliances.

At all events, we four had a very sympathetic, always encouraging childhood. There were certain real sexual repressions in the air, yet my memory tells me that the concept of life as rare and enjoyable—full of delicious moments, hours, and full days—was certainly made very clear to us in those less stressful times, simply because of all that we were offered, did, and loved. The swimming, croquet, kite-flying, softball, and thirty-six-mile ice-skating trips on Winnebago's smooth black ice.

Molly, Robert, Phyllis, and Chandler

Mr. Radford would take the four of us on the Interurban to Neenah, where, strapping on skates and sometimes unfurling homemade sails, we covered the length of the lake, free as birds. Then we'd cook lunch on father's island, The Fraction, pack up, and set out again, to arrive six miles farther south at Fond du Lac, where we'd catch the next swaying Interurban car back to Oshkosh. There, we would disembark at the station and limp home with the now heavy skates to fall into bed.

With Mrs. Radford's money, Mr. Radford bought an elm-covered island eight miles north of Oshkosh and a quarter of a mile from the mainland. On it were ten summer cottages, a caretaker's house, and a central dining hall.

We visited the two young daughters and the parents for a week each summer. There was a great deal of fishing, swimming, swinging in a frightening thirty-foot-high rope swing, and walking around the island's perimeters. The four of us children stopped sometimes on a small sand beach to gather colored stones and eroded bricks, which we pounded with rocks into colored powders, carefully put in empty clam shells, and then traded and bartered—the common colors for the rarer.

23

Then came the afternoon swim. Molly swam like a fish and even crossed the quarter-mile channel, urged on by proud Mr. Radford in a rowboat. I learned the dog paddle when Mrs. Radford tied a line about my middle, fastened it to the end of a bamboo fishing pole, and walked up and down the big wooden dock set on its driven piles eight feet above me, calling down instructions as I slowly got the hang of it. Being fat, I floated easily, but I was not an athlete.

We would also "think up" plays and produce them for the older people, who watched from the broad wooden porches that surrounded each cottage.

A large, white, mahogany-enclosed launch used to transport local families out for the summer and bring the husbands out after work each afternoon. It tied up at the high, weathered dock overnight and departed for Oshkosh the next morning at seven-thirty.

Mr. Radford's various schemes—such as planting sugar beets or importing Holland bulbs—to run the island at a profit gradually came to nothing and the place fell into decay.

* * *

Chandler was far brighter than I. It has always seemed to me a great pity that he did not end up at the University of Wisconsin teaching economics. Yet, being second-born, and hence, less put upon by uncertain parents, I was able to enjoy life more. I was more open to feelings than to discreet systems of thought.

For me, the whole learning process was free of

Sail skating

pressure—from kindergarten in the Oshkosh Normal School under Miss Henly, on through Miss Boucher, Miss Marvin, and Miss Bromberg, the olive-skinned gym teacher.

On Sunday afternoons there were family drives out into the flat, fertile farmlands surrounding Oshkosh. Our 1915 open Packard was an enormous, lumbering four-cylinder with two jump seats.

Chandler and I were allowed to choose, as guests on these outings, our favorite teachers of the moment. I always chose Miss Bromberg, and managed to get squashed in between her and the rear seat's plump leather armrest. Why I remember the positioning is hard to say, but I do, and I could draw it today. I would pretend to fall asleep after about half an hour and, instead of behaving myself, I would slowly collapse against Miss Bromberg, remaining there and sensing her warmth until the trip's end. It was pretty furtive on my part, but at least I knew what I enjoyed and, in this case, I dared to pursue it.

Miss Bromberg in bloomers

* * *

Once, in the second grade, I drew—by some stroke of luck—a black, orange, and chalk-white tiger on that cheap, well-toothed, fawn-colored paper we all were dealt. Warm and encouraging Miss Boucher said, "Robert, how did you know that the tiger's shoulder went that way?"

My observations grew increasingly perceptive after that remark.

As a child, I used to mix up various watercolor "drinks"—chocolate, lime, lemon, orange, raspberry—and then, gathering five or six peers around me, I would drink them before their eyes. Pure insecure fat-boy bravado on my part—but their eyeballs doubled in size.

I also became very good at casting hand shadows on a wall, particularly in front of my beloved Magic Lantern. It was hot as Tophet and smelled of burnt tin, but it threw a great white rectangle on any wall. I discovered early that I could produce laughs with various accompanying talk, quacking sounds, peeps, squeaks, and murmurs.

Of course, in a low-key way, all of this was reinforcing and calling upon my imagination. Unfortunately, I was also beginning to be the small fat boy who couldn't

Impersonating Chaplin at nine

run very fast or swim too well, and consequently I was having to learn to be funny—both to gain attention and so that I would be laughed with rather than at.

We had to go to dancing school each Saturday morning in the U.S. Armory. The whole scheme wrecked our one free day. We were forced to wear dark blue coats, knickers, and white gloves, and to carry a white handkerchief to place decorously against the young ladies' backs as we lurched uncertainly through those stilted steps.

As one boy later remarked, "All the girls were so strong."

*   *   *

We built enormous box kites, some six feet long and covered with cloth. There were some fanciful ones, too, and I put faces on mine, and often arms and legs.

On any windy day in summer four or five of us would gather at the Buckstaff house or at our house. I was the youngest, for they were generally Chandler's friends. Mounting our bicycles, we would set off like some destroyer flotilla for the old golf club, just south of town and across the Fox River. The clubhouse was wide-porched, two stories high, and enclosed one large, unpretentious room for rainy-night meals when the verandas and the incredible summer sunsets were denied. The outside was painted white; the inside entirely varnished and yellowing with age. It was on the grounds there that we flew our latest creations.

One day, clinging to the winder of a monster kite in a stiff wind, I sensed, to my horror, that I was being dragged across the open field. Had I let go of the line the kite would have settled to earth and been retrieved intact. But instead, fearing the shouting scorn of the older boys, I clung to the twine and was slowly dragged by the powerful kite toward a five-foot hedgerow. I attempted to leap into the air to clear it but instead was hauled right through, and was badly scratched. Lying on my stomach crying, I watched the kite slowly wobble down an eighth of a mile away.

It was during kite time that my mother returned from Chicago with thirty-two feet of quarter-inch-square rubber for the model planes I was beginning to build. Little did I realize that she had spent an entire day tracking it down.

* * *

Anyone who has ever received one of my letters knows that, for me, spelling has been a steadily deepening jungle, a miasmic swamp, ever since that totally illogical alphabet—with its silly syllables, pronunciations, and trick-laden sounds—entered my early world.

Drawn from six or more other languages, then melded into one English spelling book, it is hirled, herled, hurled at unsuspecting children by teachers who come in once a week and attempt to weld SPELLING to the lower back of the brain.

In deepening despair, those teachers would phone mother to say that Robert somehow wasn't grasping the principles. And, of course, when I pointed out that when one or more rules didn't work, they said, "Oh! That is an exception." The whole scheme was obviously shot through with festering exceptions and lack of order. Yet, I noticed as a young boy that the leaf of an hepatica, or the wings of green- or blue-winged teal never presented an exception. Teal's wings were always clear, totally logical, the color exact—and in every case memorable. Not so with words!

I write all this in considerable indignation, for as a youngster I was made to feel, both by adults and by my peers, that if I couldn't even learn to *spell* there wasn't much hope for me—perhaps a sawmill job where I would probably cut off my left hand.

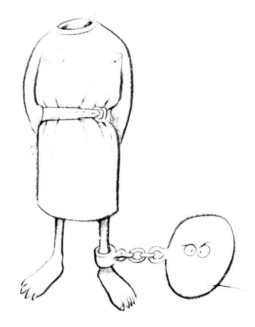

Poor speller

* * *

I found Mrs. Hollister, the mother of my friend Seymour, very attractive. She and her equally striking sister had come to Oshkosh from Buffalo as young women. Quite unlike the plump stingless Wasps I grew up with, she was totally unconventional.

Often after school Seymour, black-bearded at thirteen, and I would walk the mile and a half to his home, where we'd sprawl out on the thick white rug in Mr. Hollister's study and listen in blinding ecstasy to George Gershwin's *Rhapsody in Blue* played by Paul Whiteman's band, time after 78-rpm-needle-bending time. No one said, "Boys, haven't you heard that stuff enough?"

At some point Mrs. Hollister would come down the white, ballustraded, scarlet-carpeted staircase, her pei-

With my box Brownie

Mrs. Hollister

gnoir flowing and noticeably parting. She would pass us, smile, lift her long ivory cigarette holder and inhale, the cigarette tip glowing suddenly brighter—then she would turn from us and go out to talk to the cook.

It was pretty heady stuff, even for Slow Learner—particularly the draft of perfume as she passed Seymour and me. It shortened my breath.

Some time later, Mrs. Hollister shortened her own breath by closing the garage doors tightly behind their running Buick. The thought of this once seductive woman foundering as she was confronted by early middle age saddened me.

* * *

To impress my father, I bought a complete football outfit at the Fulton Gun Store. One warm afternoon during practice, taunted by the coach, I tackled Jack Nusbaum, the first-team captain, straight on. Charlotte Chase and Seymour Hollister were watching from the sidelines. I promptly threw up, lying stunned on the grass, and I felt dizzy for the next twenty-four hours. I soon gave up football even though the school cheer was "We will fight until we die for Oshkosh High, the school of the pink and the green. . . ."

* * *

There were gentle moments in all seasons. Fall picnics in strange fields beneath harvest moons, with kind friends four or five years older than I and already in college, heading for M.I.T., or in love with young men at Harvard. I was bolstered by the fact that they invited me into their more intense and sophisticated circle, for I was getting nowhere at all with the girls of my own age—unlike my more fortunate peers!

Ellen Gould, four years older than I, was a superb jazz pianist. Her nose was somewhat snubbed, but she was full of zest and vitality. When I was in high school, she would invite me to her house, and there play jazz to me for hours.

It was her father, Harry Gould, who hired Alexander Calder to come out to Oshkosh and design wooden toys for his failing sash and door factory. Using their scraps, Calder made a kangaroo, a bucking cow, a waddling duck, and a skating bear.

Ellen Gould's friend, Eleanor Chase, lived across the street from us in a gigantic, four-story-high "Dutch" house. Eleanor was beautiful in an F. Scott Fitzgerald way: enormous blue eyes, exquisite legs, quite tall and, best of all, for all of us out there in the wastelands, she was writing well enough to be published in New York. In those days I was sending imitation Ferenc Molnár short pieces to *Vanity Fair*, detailing my triangular miseries and failures with handsome Seymour and spellbinding Charlotte Chase. The magazine's editor, Frank Crownin-shield, would send his exquisitely printed rejection slip only after writing on it, "We cannot use this, but keep sending in more. F.C." That was all I needed to plow ahead, nostrils well above the oncoming waves and undertow.

A bit later, Ellen and Eleanor took up with Robert Benchley and Marc Connelly at the Algonquin Hotel in far-away New York. When Connelly, an ebullient, totally delightful man, came out to Oshkosh for a visit, Eleanor asked me over for dinner. I found this pretty heady stuff and practically stripped the gears telling funny stories about duck shooting and whatever else I could cook up in my young brain at that moment. Eleanor told me later that Connelly thought I was funny. Again, a piton of sorts had been set. It encouraged me.

A Sunday afternoon drive in our carriage

JOYS OF THE COUNTRY

Duck shooting with first gun

Living in Wisconsin, and at an early age, I was constantly exposed to the joys of the country. My love for it, as opposed to the excitement of the city, has clearly governed my life. The country has always seemed less concocted, more resourceful in its own right than that which human beings put together, too often in the sand-grinding bearings of their minds alone, with insufficient heart.

In Oshkosh we had the outdoors—for fishing, swimming, skating, riding, shooting, boating, and hiking. We built things with our two hands and simple tools; we made our own skis from barrel staves, drew, and did watercolors. By comparison, today's values seem jumbled—the choices offered are complex indeed, the objectives so often muddled. No wonder it is much harder for young people to search their way through the often threatening times and environment. The open meadows, the silence of the woods and their uncomplicated streams rarely appear accessible.

* * *

We lived not far from Lake Winnebago, the largest body of fresh water entirely within the United States. It provided great shooting and fishing, and even had sturgeon, which provided their own indistinctive caviar. The sailboat racing, in scow-bottom, twenty-eight-foot boats, was tricky in sudden storms but very fast. Under just the right "reaching" conditions we once did one three-and-a-half-mile leg of a race at a speed of twenty-eight knots. I sailed in a crew of five with John Buckstaff, a highly competent, and very competitive skipper. He also built and sailed a forty-foot iceboat carrying an enormous amount of sail, in which he traveled one hundred and twenty-two miles an hour on a straightaway nine-mile run. Each year we went for a week-long regatta on Lake Geneva in Wisconsin or Lake Minnetonka in Minnesota, and every third year the races were held at the Oshkosh Yacht Club.

Jack Ordway, Leonard Carpenter, and a Mr. Kimberly from Neenah were the exceptional skippers. Phil Pillsbury, a plump Yale undergraduate, was used for ballast on the Ordway boat. Like galley slaves, we amateur crews were forced to stand way out on the upwind bilge boards to bring the windward rail of the boat down so we wouldn't capsize, and also to afford these very elegant boats greater thrust.

One noon, a traveling salesman from Chicago, standing at the bar of the Hotel Athearn, fell into conversation with two or three local ice yachtsmen. He was arguing that no boat could go faster than the wind. "It's impossible!"

Fortified with firewater, the poor fellow became obstreperous as he talked about how and why boats move. Finally, the local sailors said, "Well, let's go down to the lake, it's only six blocks away—it won't take but a minute—and we can go out for a ride. The wind is fairly good and the ice is really clear."

The "city boy" put on his Chesterfield and fedora and was soon loaded into the roomy open cockpit, with Buckstaff at the tiller. They were given a shove and away they went.

The wind's speed was quickly surpassed and soon they were doing sixty or seventy miles per hour. Back at the yacht club, the salesman's stiffened form was lifted out by his arms and legs, much as one would lift stretched frozen muskrat skins. He was revived back at the Athearn bar and no one was mean enough to inform him that that very boat could go much faster, indeed had averaged over one hundred and twenty miles per hour.

* * *

On the way to The Fraction

Father was happiest when out of doors. He enjoyed, and was good at, fishing for trout and the enormous forty- and fifty-pound muskellunge. He was a better than average partridge, prairie chicken, and duck shot.

About 1908 he wisely bought a small, low island in the southern section of Lake Winnebago, nine miles north of Fond du Lac. It was called The Fraction, why exactly I don't know. He also bought, a bit later, some nearby marshy shoreland and another small island called The Willows. These lands afforded some seven duck blinds from which one could shoot in almost any wind, with the decoys clearly visible in calm water.

Over open water we shot redhead, widgeon, pintail, and greater and lesser scaup, which we called blue-bills—a more descriptive and less ugly word. But most interesting of all were the canvasbacks: handsome, large, delicious to eat, and almost as canny as any of the mallards and the few blacks we saw.

The fulcrum for all of us shooting out there was Fred Abrams, a farmer of sorts, but above all, a truly crafty duck hunter and an incredibly gifted shot. As a boy I once saw him drop five blue-winged teal, one after another, with his old and battered Winchester pump, as they streaked by the east end of The Fraction, barely in range.

In his narrow, pale olive-green skiff, totally exposed in open water and knowing that father and Chandler and I were watching him, he would drift down upon two Canadian geese. Using one slowly protruded hand to starboard and another to port, he would keep the skiff in the concealing glare of the sun's water path until at last, in sure range, he would rise suddenly to his knees, gun in hand, and as the geese rose he would drop them both, pick them up, and then, paddle swiftly back to the blind, obviously, yet modestly, pleased as we three amateurs stood shouting praise.

We always enjoyed going down to the Abrams' farm the night before, either in a carriage or, later, in a roomy four-cylinder car.

Fred's wife, Della, always got up at about 3:30 A.M. to start breakfast and to rout all of us out of the three upstairs bedrooms—heated mostly by our bodies in the feather beds. Full of anticipation, we would stumble down the narrow, steep staircase into the kitchen, with its three pools of yellow light beneath three ugly oil lamps. Set upon the long white oilcloth table, and ready to be consumed, were fried potatoes, fried eggs, fried bacon, hot oatmeal, fresh cream, and muffins.

Then, in the still or sometimes windy darkness, warm within from the hearty breakfasts, we would carefully shuffle across the frost-white lawn to the long, flimsy two-plank pier, where we'd discreetly lower ourselves into the thirty-foot open launch. Fred would bring the immense two-lunger engine to life, nearly casting his right shoulder out of its concave joint in the process, and we would set off, skiffs in tow, toward the blinds Fred had, in his instinctive heart, chosen for that morning's shooting.

In the oncoming dawn he would set the fifty decoys with a knowledge and deftness that was a joy to watch. His ability to bring in the different ducks with various calls which he'd learned as a young boy, using nothing but his lips and his cupped hands, was pure magic. We all admired this particular ability, but it was his timing of anything he thought necessary that made him such an exceptional guide.

Later, back home, I would go up three stories to my carefully painted salmon-pink "studio" to try to set down and somewhat redeem the birds' loss of life—the Wilson snipe, the canvasback, and even one eider duck that father unwittingly shot.

Unfortunately, as the years wore on, Fred Abrams drank more and more locally brewed beer. Finally, one afternoon he forgot to come out in the big launch through a gale-force wind to recover father and his friends from The Fraction. They all spent an entire November night in the leeward east blind. Fred, sobered up, showed up the next morning to take them back across the open water to shore. No one spoke a word until they docked—when Fred was promptly and empathetically fired on the long rickety pier. All of this was very hard on Della, who already looked very much like Dorothea Lange's photograph of that spent sharecropper's wife.

* * *

When I was old enough to be trusted not to kill anyone with my "410," or later, with an exquisitely engraved, shoulder-whacking, double-barreled twelve-gauge (which I never liked), father would take me along on any partridge or prairie chicken shooting expedition.

Once we two had traveled by Soo Line train to Marshfield or Medford, there was extraordinary shooting to be had at the various lumber camps or along the hedgerows and open fields.

One spring father bought a large liver-spotted pointer. All that summer he worked assiduously out on the front lawn teaching Duke to heel, sit, charge, and to retrieve a canvas dummy and deposit it at father's feet.

With the arrival of fall father set off with Duke for the first hunt. Imagine his dismay on discovering that Duke had no "nose"—no sense of scents or odors. He would walk over birds and be as surprised as they were as they burst into the air. Poor Duke became a handsome and excused house pet.

Another pleasure I enjoyed with father was our trout-fishing expeditions in the northern woods. If we did not go to Lake Gogebic we would board a single railroad car that was attached to a long line of freight cars. Leather seats were placed along its sides, and above us, on the ceiling's curvature, was a long, hand-painted oil mural of rising trout, sulking muskellunge, and vicious-looking smallmouth bass beneath plenty of lily pads.

The trip to Cavour took eleven hours, during which we would go through a hamper of food and many cribbage games before descending, finally, at a minute station. From there we walked a quarter of a mile to a small farmhouse set beside a perfect trout stream, where we would stay for three or four days in those simple and unstressed times.

Houseboat at Butte des Morts

PLANES AND CARS

Two of my early loves were planes and cars. I'm still excited by almost any airplane or hydroplane, against almost any sky, but best of all were the early planes with wings you could see through and engines, spun or fixed, which you could barely hear.

One Sunday I rode my solid Crescent bicycle to the fairgrounds to see Mr. Charles Frank Niles's Moisant monoplane being assembled. It had been brought from Milwaukee on a flatcar and was to perform that afternoon.

I was mesmerized, for I had built a blue silk three-foot Blériot model very similar to the Moisant. Mine had made a thirteen-foot flight ending in a crumpling dive. Later that day I saw Niles attain about one thousand feet and then, to the horror of the gasping, gawking crowd, the starboard wing simply separated from the fragile longeron and the plane turned into a steeper and steeper right-hand dive. I could see the terror-stricken pilot from the ground. The severed wing, slowly revolving, glided away to the north.

The crowd rushed out of the stands toward the wreck. I was sickened by the sight of people pulling even the cuff links from the dead pilot's shirt. I didn't dare tell my family what I'd seen and went to bed early.

I would have expected that, as I matured, my enjoyment of and admiration for airplanes would have slowly decreased. On the contrary, my interest in them, even in their principles, seems endless, beginning with those two very American geniuses, the Wright brothers. Blessed with uninhibited reasoning and imagining processes, they finally understood flight, and solved problems that had previously prevented *controllable* flight. They were middle-western in all of their habits and practices, and certainly Gemini geniuses nearly beyond belief.

The most brilliant pilot I ever encountered was a flyer in France named Dorêt. He flew a high-wing De-

monoplan Antoinette. 1909 french

Osborn

woitine at the summer air shows at Vincennes between 1932 and 1937.

Coming in over the field at very high speed, he would use a short, small hook bound into the tip of the right wing to pick up a bunched-up white handkerchief from the grass and then, still at full throttle, go straight up and do above us a stunning set of flowing and imaginative acrobatics. At the end, the handkerchief, finally torn free, descended peacefully, like some slow-motion bridal bouquet.

The whole performance was obviously dangerous. We all sensed this, yet Dorêt was such an incredibly accurate and responsive pilot that he could compensate instantly for the slightest change in either wing's lift or loss of it.

"Wind sheer" as a hazard was not even known in those days. However, Dorêt probably dreamed about it.

Cars also possessed a fascination for me, and still do—from father's early open Packards, with their ponderous four cylinders, gas-burning headlamps, totally undependable tires, built-in rear trunks holding four

36

dust-proof touring suitcases, and engine hand cranks that could easily break your right arm if they unexpectedly "kicked back"; to the later dumpy-looking Cadillacs, and Choate Brown's Pierce-Arrow with its handsome solution for headlights. Also there was Oshan Waite's open Marmon—very fast for those days—and Dr. Clarke's slope-fronted, air-cooled Franklin, which I stole for twenty minutes one Saturday night and raced at full throttle up and down Algoma Street while the adults were occupied with their cards at the West End Whist Club.

My friends in Neenah, John and Barbara Babcock, each owned a two-seater Daniels car. We traveled at speeds approaching ninety miles an hour on those narrow, deserted macadam roads between Neenah and Oshkosh. Why we all weren't killed, I still don't know. Actually, Chandler smashed up one Cadillac, and drove another down into a grassy ditch and then back up onto the road because he had the windshield turned down and at fifty miles an hour his eyelids fluttered so badly he couldn't see where he was going. I was clinging to the car's leather seat. When we were back up on the macadam, proceeding toward the new Pau-Ka-Tuk Country Club, south of Oshkosh, he made me promise not to tell father what had happened. I promised, still shaken, and with that settled we went out and played eighteen holes of golf. Altogether, I was in six car accidents before I was twenty-two. They were frequent occurrences in the hinterlands in that period.

Oshkosh had two of those superbly designed early Dusenbergs. The Paines had Stanley Steamers that the chauffeur preheated. Harry Gould drove a twelve-cylinder Packard, too fast. The cars were all impressive, carefully built, and beautifully painted.

The head of the Diamond Match Company in Oshkosh used to drive over poor and narrow roads to Indianapolis each year to see the July Fourth Five-Hundred-Mile Race. He was killed while returning home one year. I regretted it for some time, because he used to draw and color, before his son's eyes and mine, wild Indians on racing ponies with the usual distended nostrils and stuck-out eyeballs.

Later, in France, there were the elegant Delahayes and the two-seater open Hispanos at the Hotel Eden Roc—very erotic objects. Mercedes, even in those days, were cursed with that strange Germanic heaviness that they seem unable to escape. All of the Rolls and Bentleys took one's breath away. The front fenders sprang forward with a vital grace, and you knew that these cars were perfectly put together by serious craftsmen. There was none of the ponderous pomposity of the present day products.

The Bugattis—and they were not uncommon in those days in France—appeared slowly and with extraordinary care from the Molsheim plant of Ettore Bugatti. They had one problem: they were so exquisite in all details that one needed an impeccable mechanic in the enormous tool kit to keep them firing and running properly. However, what man, before or since, has designed and built such astonishingly interesting machines as those of Ettore Bugatti, that horseshoe-laden, ebullient fat man in a fawn-colored derby?

I still own a 1951 two-and-a-half-liter "drophead" Riley, with a hand-hammered aluminum body and lines only a capable artist could have devised.

ON WISCONSIN

It is hard to convey the aesthetic isolation I felt during my last years in Oshkosh. Hence, my subscriptions to *The Dial* and *Vanity Fair* magazines were extremely important to me. I used to sit out on the front steps, aged sixteen or so, awaiting the postman on the days they were to appear.

They were lucky forces in my life, but *The Dial* was the stronger. It was in its pages that I first encountered Cézanne. As I came to appreciate his work, I would sometimes get up at 4:00 A.M., walk down silent Algoma Street, catch the train to Chicago, and spend the late morning at the Art Institute looking at the Seurat and the Gauguins, but above all at Cézanne's *View from L'Estaque*, which simply bowled me over. It was a totally new experience and I sensed that the emotions it evoked were different from those given by pictures I had been exposed to earlier. In the afternoon I could see plays such as the Moscow Art Theatre's *The Lower Depths*, or *Liliom*, and then catch the 5:30 train back to Oshkosh.

In 1923, I entered the University of Wisconsin. Everyone I knew went there. Your parents paid $16.50 for the year. You couldn't be refused if you came from Wisconsin. Everyone knew that you had to get an "education"; that was what one did. So naturally, with no escapes, one pressed happily onward, ever upward, and one was encouraged to learn at every point—from those first kind spinstresses, through an arid stretch of mediocre teaching in high school, to the first year at Wisconsin.

There, two excellent things happened to me. One, by pure chance I had a first-rate young English teacher, Miss Dwyer, a very small but radiant person. She encouraged me in the way I was combining drawings with writing.

Two, Professor Frank Jewett Mather came from Princeton to lecture in Bascom Hall on Impressionism and Postimpressionism. As he spoke in a scholarly way to one slide after another of Monet, Pissaro, Renoir,

Tolstoy's Dolokhof, drawn in 1923

39

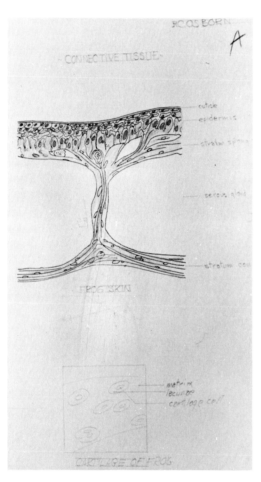

Drawing for zoology lab

Seurat, and Cézanne, I suddenly saw a whole new world—different from the large sepia print of Corot at home beside the Steinway. For me, it was an enormous step forward, taken alone.

As I walked down the long sloping hill from Bascom Hall back into reality, the dusk was upon everything and snowflakes—clearly separated—were slowly falling. In a genuine ecstasy I was overcome by this latest revelation and the moment.

Clive Bell, and soon Roger Fry, were to make this new perception and revitalization of painting even clearer to me.

As a freshman at Wisconsin I ran the low hurdles until the coach remarked that I had long legs and moved me to the high hurdles. At first it went well, but then one afternoon I nicked the top crossbar and went sprawling—planing down the black cinder track on my palms and knees as the empennage settled. For several years my hands still showed the specks of black beneath the skin.

I did well in an interesting course in zoology, mainly because of my drawing, and ended the year with an overall average of ninety-two. However, I also had acquired a fullblown duodenal ulcer. It was decided that I would spend the next year at home and go to the Presbyterian–St. Luke Hospital in Chicago under Dr. Sippy, the top ulcer specialist in the country. Just having him stand at the foot of my bed each morning had a healing effect.

There was also an Irish nurse by the name of Fenna Van Vessen who interested me as Miss Bromberg had. I suspect that I also interested her, for she would come in around ten in the evening and sit on my bed and talk. It was the most gentle of love affairs, even in memory.

YALE AND TO EUROPE

After that year at home and in the Chicago Presbyterian Hospital, I wrote letters to Yale. My grades at Wisconsin apparently impressed them in those easy-going days for I did not have to pass their exams, and so in the autumn of 1924 I was once again a freshman, this time in New Haven. It was the beginning of the really helpful years, though at the time I didn't sense it.

Fine teachers spent a great deal of effort trying to inspire us. John Archer Gee, unduly fat, talked about Sir John Falstaff on warm spring afternoons in Berkeley Hall, and no one dozed; and Francis Bangs, my proctor, spent endless hours describing the joys of New York and Long Island ladies and general dalliance, but also introduced me to the glories of Dante.

By the time Christmas came around I was having such a great time that I didn't go home. Instead, I bought tickets for almost two steady weeks of matinee and evening performances in the New York theatres. I would draw a picture showing that I disliked being placed directly behind any post, send it in with my two dollars— and get ideal seats every time. I stayed at a stuffy Alpha Delta Phi Club where old members fumbled around at chess, and I spent Christmas Eve in a small timbered restaurant (Dickensian for me) in Greenwich Village, the streets white with snow. The proprietress was most solicitous of this single man who in fact was perfectly happy.

Spring vacation I remained in New Haven reading all of Dante's writings. On bright days I went by trolley to Mt. Carmel and read all day in the fields there, until one afternoon I spotted an enormous snake slowly coming down the apple tree's trunk directly overhead. On rainy days I simply lay on my bed reading *De Monarchia* or whatever and smoking, by this time, Cubebs—very heavy, very satisfactory Turkish cigarettes which came in very refined boxes.

My intake of "knowledge" in those years was enor-

The Yale RECORD

Yale Record *board. I am sitting front row, second from left, next to Dwight MacDonald, Geoffrey Hellman, Wilder Hobson, horn.*

mous; the psyche's more basic demands would insist on other needs later.

The insights of two other teachers at Yale meant a great deal to me: Robert French, who taught Chaucer, giving us a life-long love of that extraordinary poet, joker, and observant realist; and Alexander Witherspoon, who was able to convey a sense of the continuum of any culture—from Cro-Magnon or Celtic man to Miró. He'd employ any means, from eighteenth-century English broadsides to the Armory Show catalogue, to get us to think a bit. It was heady teaching, and four of us blessed souls in Witherspoon's chosen group used to prepare for each class together until 2 A.M., uttering in the meantime a great deal of pure nonsense. And then, cold-sober, we would all go off to our rooms to sleep, contentedly anticipating the next surprise to be sprung by Witherspoon's agile and inquiring mind.

One exasperating experience was my attempt to get into a freehand drawing class at the Yale Art School. I'd taken mechanical drawing to avoid calculus, which simply reduced my brain to a boggled custard. At the end of that freshman year I appealed to a very fat, jovial Dean Meeks to let me take the course. A year passed. Another year passed. Finally Meeks said that I could enter Dietrickson's class, on Tuesdays and Thursdays from two to four, in depressingly gloomy Weir Hall. I was ecstatic. I bought Ingres paper, fifty sticks of charcoal, a Chardin-like charcoal holder, a grey kneaded eraser, and a large black portfolio with three tie-together ribbons. I was now, at last, an *artist*.

The first week Dietrickson said that we would draw that usual, featureless, dead-white plaster cast head to be found in every art school in those days. We all did. By the end of the week my paper was turning brown from erasing burnt charcoal. Surely next week would be more interesting, a nude or something. The next Tuesday Herr Dietrickson announced we would continue working on the "head" we had started. I couldn't believe it. I worked for about an hour on the faceless face, turning it ever browner and finally, with no modesty or humility, I gleefully added George Bernard Shaw's satanic eyebrows, an upturned moustache, and a pointed beard. Dietrickson soon approached, glowered down at my drawing, and said, "Young man, I don't think we need your type here. You may leave."

I picked up all of my newly bought "artist" materials, tied up my three-string portfolio and, wending my way between the wooden easels, departed.

Later, and one mustn't be too prickly about this, I was chairman for six years of the Yale Art and Architecture Alumni Council, following Eero Saarinen. We brought that great teacher Josef Albers into the school and the institution took off into a disciplined, varied direction, exploring all aspects of line, color, form, and space. Never have I seen an art school such as that at Yale under Albers. No longer were superb colors converted day after day into that horrid dung color which is the

The plaster head, improved

hallmark of all art schools. Effective art and architecture schools come and go, like morels in the spring, almost unpredictably: the Bauhaus with Gropius, Kandinsky, Klee, Breuer, Bayer, Albers, Anni Albers, and Moholy-Nagy; Black Mountain with Albers and Schawinsky; Harvard's School of Architecture under Gropius and Breuer; Chicago's School of Design under Moholy-Nagy; Harvard's Carpenter Center with Sert and Robert Gardner; the Yale School of Architecture with Louis Kahn. . . . They appear, fade drastically, yet can reappear. In Paris, Léger, Matisse, Despiau, Friesz, Jeanneret, and Derain revived small schools with their inspiring Friday morning critiques.

It should be added that much later the Yale Arts Association awarded me their medal for "distinction in the visual arts." Designed by Albers, it is a very handsome medal and I was touched by the kindness of the association's artists and architects.

* * *

Our days at Yale were pleasant, harmless, padded, unreal, and yet we were learning the areas of cultivation from which we have ever since drawn our delights and the comprehension of our time. And this is really what any lively college can give, be it Yale, Harvard, Berkeley, Oxford, Cambridge, or the Sorbonne in Paris. The fields of cultivation are indicated and, as one learns that they exist, one senses that they can be enjoyed and used in the articulation of oneself.

* * *

Dwight MacDonald, Wilder Hobson, Geoffrey Hellman, Jack Jessup, and I published the puerile *Yale Record* and we were all taken into the Elizabethan Club at various points. It was the club I most enjoyed at Yale. We had tea every afternoon and some pretty esoteric conversations with such men as Chauncey Brewster Tinker, Thornton Wilder, and Sam Hemingway.

When father wrote that he had been completely reduced by the Depression and could send no more money, I began to draw all sorts of ads at five dollars a drawing.

I also sent the *New Yorker* cartoons with captions, and Harold Ross would send back typewritten pages telling me what was wrong with each one and what to pursue. At one point I sent him a drawing of two trapeze artists in which one has just missed his partner, who is clearly falling. There is no net. The caption was "Oops, sorry!" Ross bought the line and had a man named Shanks draw it. James Thurber told me later that Ross had always said, "Now, *that* is the kind of situation and line that I want in the *New Yorker.*"

I was shaken at having my drawing turned down. But I took my five dollar payment for the joke. Actually, Ross was trying to make me into a gag cartoonist, which I began to sense that I was not. I did sell one drawing to the *New Yorker*; it was about a flea trainer.

In those last years at Yale I worked for the *New Haven Register* as a caricaturist, and one day I was told to go to the Taft Hotel to draw Katharine Cornell, who was playing at the Schubert Theatre in *The Barretts of Wimpole Street*. I was delighted, for I had one of those crushes young men develop. I rushed over to the Taft, paper and pencil in hand.

I phoned up from the front desk. Yes, she was in her room. She probably added that she would come down, but I leapt into the elevator and was promptly knocking on her door. We were both surprised. She was in a dark red silk kimono. "I didn't expect you up here," she said. "I was going to come down . . . but you might as well make the drawing here."

Thoroughly flustered, I began to draw. The second sketch was no better than the first, and so they went. At the end of about twenty minutes—without showing her the ten drawings which in no way resembled any one of her very special features—I said, "Oh! These are just sketches to work from," thanked her, and backed out of the room. I did promise to send her the newspaper later.

Once back in the Harkness dormitory I began the winnowing and refining process but nothing happened whatsoever. Occasionally a certain resemblance would begin to emerge, only to evaporate as I pursued that tack in the next drawing.

I did one hundred and eight drawings and finally, in a complete quandry, took one down to the *Register*. I needed the five dollars. They did print it but I didn't send a copy to Cornell. Instead I wrote her some effusive fan-

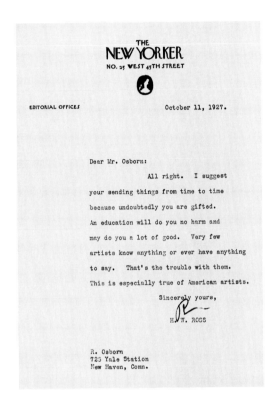

THE
NEW YORKER
NO. 25 WEST 45TH STREET

EDITORIAL OFFICES   October 11, 1927.

Dear Mr. Osborn:

         All right. I suggest
your sending things from time to time
because undoubtedly you are gifted.
An education will do you no harm and
may do you a lot of good. Very few
artists know anything or ever have anything
to say. That's the trouble with them.
This is especially true of American artists.

                    Sincerely yours,

                    H. W. ROSS

R. Osborn
725 Yale Station
New Haven, Conn.

Katharine Cornell

46

tasy about how her coming to New Haven had had the same effect on the undergraduate body that Zuleika Dobson had had upon . . . etc., etc.

When I met her later in Minneapolis, I reminded her of the incident. She remembered it. "You seemed quite nervous. Even the pencil shook."

* * *

One May day in 1927, we all learned in the papers that Lindbergh had taken off at 7:52 A.M. to cross the Atlantic single-handed. Anyone with any sense knew that he was hanging his life on the performance of one fairly reliable radial engine. He knew it too.

As the hours wore on, the strange collective excitement mounted. By 10:00 A.M. the next morning, vague reports began to come in that he was crossing Ireland and then England. By then the enclosed campus was filling with hundreds of students just standing there quietly in the morning warmth, waiting. Then, like a rifle shot, a third-story window slammed up, a mouth opened and screamed: "He's made it! He's in Paris!" The last phrase was drowned by the roar which rose from the crowd like some exploding balloon of joy.

With that straightforward, decent, youthful face, his modesty, and his extraordinary flying abilities, Lindbergh at once became a welcome national hero and, slowly, a symbol of achievement to the world. His later misuse of that position was saddening to watch.

* * *

After Yale, which was far better for me than my ego understood at the time, I left for Rome via London and Paris, with $1500 I had earned by drawing. I went by boat, *The American Farmer*, in the early fall to London. The ten-day passage cost one hundred dollars.

The second day out, I accidentally threw overboard our one piece of amusement equipment—a heavy leather medicine ball. I watched it hit the wooden port rail, roll along for twenty feet, and tumble down the steamer's side into the vast Atlantic. For the rest of the unamused voyage many of the passengers sneered at me, except for two prim young nurses going to Europe for the first time.

I found London very sympathetic. I stayed at Rosa Lewis's Cavendish Hotel. The whole Anglo-Saxon culture that I had studied for the last four years was there. I

Lindbergh's lonely flight

had even taken with me my treasured Arthur Rackham's *Peter Pan in Kensington Gardens*, and I used to sit at twilight in Kensington Garden or in the broader Hyde Park, basking in it all. Everything was exactly as that excellently trained artist drew it. I wrote my family ecstatic letters. I ordered two suits at Anderson and Sheppard, one of which I've never found the equal of and both of which I still have and wear on occasion. And because I had been studying for four years, I was able to absorb and remember facts, scenes, and impressions like some ready sponge. My sentimental, imitative diary doesn't reflect this but I know now that it was true.

From London I sent my steamer trunk off to Rome and headed for Paris. Twelve of us took off from Croydon Airfield, the women in those long linen dusters worn for motoring. The plane was a Handley Page twin-engined biplane. The longerons showed through the fabric of the fuselage, as did the ribs through the two varnished wings. Once airborne it was a slow, relatively safe plane. We never exceeded four hundred feet in altitude, and once across the grey lizard skin of the Channel, France's exquisitely honed landscape flowed beneath us. We put down at Le Bourget, where Lindbergh had landed, and were driven into Paris. I got a very cheap room four and a half floors up in the narrow Hotel Vendôme, but from my oval window I could look out on the Place Vendôme, that miracle of contained formality.

The staff at the Cavendish, Rosa Lewis at right

ROME AND PARIS

I spent four days in Paris, eating mostly chocolate because it was the only French word I could pronounce surely, then took a train to Chartres, where I was completely overcome by that cathedral, seen first under a full moon. After two days there, studying it in detail and staying at a wonderfully French hotel, I bought a one-speed bicycle for twenty-eight dollars and, strapping on my one large duffle bag, set off for Toulouse along a route laid out for me by my professor of medieval art at Yale, John Allison.

The trip was arduous. It rained for eight hours nearly every day. After a week I was considering drawing a book entitled *Up France in a Bicycle*. At Toulouse I sold the torture machine for fifteen dollars and boarded a train for Rome, where I registered at the Hotel Russe and, the next day, entered the British Academy on the Via Margutta. Thanks to a nice Miss Wyndham, I was soon settled in Prince Wolkonsky's pension on the Piazza Mignanelli.

Prince Wolkonsky's ménage was a collection of some ten paying guests who, we discovered one night at dinner, could speak twenty-six different languages. Each

Up France in a bicycle

evening Wolkonsky directed the conversation from the head of the table by introducing a general subject. Each one of us could speak to it if we wished. I've always felt that one learned more and could remember far more from these conversations than from the jumbled cross-cutting, not-listening, mish-mash table talk one endures in our country.

During my nine months in Rome I learned a great deal from early Christian mosaics studied in chronological order, one church at a time, after my morning drawing class.

I saw Rome clearly as a funnel through which had flowed much of our Western culture, from Etruscan times onward. Too, in 1928 Rome was still very much like a small town. You could walk about with ease; it was quiet; people went to sleep about 9:30 P.M. And a ten-minute tram ride brought you to the city's edge, where you could walk in open country to the Villa Madama, the *campagna* of Corot, or the Villa Doria Pamphili, to do sweeping charcoal drawings on various colors of Ingres paper, which unfortunately didn't come to blows with anything one was looking at.

The very serious blemish on that period in Rome was seeing the Italians embracing the "teachings" of fascism and the simplistically explained horrors of the Ethiopian War with no qualms whatsoever, in fact, with considerable pouter-pigeon pride.

I returned to Paris in 1929. To have lived in Paris—in any state, under any conditions, on any floor, and almost any street, particularly when one was young—was in itself a superb and painless education in how life could be lived and how it could be enjoyed. It was also a cogent lesson about the meaning and uses of ORDER.

To have simply experienced the endless beauty of that great city with its first-rate architecture and created spaces would have been reason enough to be there.

And then the French people!

I have never spent much time in Germany; I don't like being with that many double-folded rear necks bespeaking a constant threat to Western culture.

Austria seemed quite different; softer, easier, less

My Roman landlord

Sketching at Amiens

guttural and aggressive. I suspected that some Italian blood had mingled there to just the right degree.

Italy, on the other hand, was too florid; the men bombastic. They cheated on their wives until all the Italian women wore turned-down corners to their mouths, like rubber stamps of disapproval.

But in Paris it was as though, for the first time, an immense gong of Reality was ringing. I am sure that my life was changed and has been determined ever since by those early adult years, four in all, in Paris and the French provinces, and by encountering those self-sufficient, self-confident people. Even today, look at the women as you pass them in the streets at noon, with their simple, yet self-understood clothes; and hear their capacity to "talk back" to their men in a most civilized fashion, as absolute equals.

* * *

In Paris there were various *académies* in which one could learn to paint. Léger ran one, Ozenfant another, in which he taught his cold, tight, almost Prussian-like theories. They were all within a long slingshot of the "Dome," Lipps, and M. Foinet's paint store. The teachers in those four or five *académies* were accomplished painters and sculptors. If the wind was right we could nearly hear Léger in his tiny one-room academy down the street from ours, haranguing his pupils about vitality and primary colors.

Our teachers must have all called one another every Thursday afternoon to say, "Could you cover for me Friday morning for the critique?" We never knew who would appear to try to help us. We were exposed to, and sometimes ground down by, seven or eight artists during the year. They were all exquisitely dressed as they marched amidst our forlorn week's work, making sharp and very intelligent remarks. I recall Matisse once speaking about the total logic of light, whether sent directly from the sun or reflected.

Despiau was very gentle. Looking at our paintings, one by one, he spoke clearly to all of us about the sensitivity of the outline, what mass is, and what it can do.

Friesz was jolly, in a very subdued way, until one day he couldn't stand to see what I had muddled onto my

Les Invalides from my Paris window

Learning to draw

canvas compared to the firm young model twenty feet away. Twisting the large gold ring on his left fourth finger he gently edged me aside, took my brushes, dipped into my paints, and said, "It should be more like this: lights on both sides of the thigh. . . . Make it rounder!"

With his right forefinger he smudged together certain meeting edges of paint until he was satisfied. Fuming, I said, "Why don't you sign it?" The class half-laughed.

However, Friesz was, all told, a good teacher—clear, logical, and pleasant, though far less sensitive than the others.

One Christmas morning we expatriates, far from home, organized a "class" with our favorite model at the Académie Scandinav to paint together and drink some wine. Friesz kindly showed up and, thanks to him, by noon the mood of the entire grey studio space was alight for all of us.

Perhaps it was that very Christmas noon that he told us a story. Rodin had agreed to look at his pictures. On the appointed morning Friesz put ten canvases into a cab and set off for Rodin's studio. The dour concierge let him in, and he set up his pictures around the walls. Presently Rodin was announced and entered. He peered at them over his stomach.

Friesz, by then, wasn't at all impressed by his paintings. They looked dingy, seemed to lack color, luminosity, almost everything. Rodin was polite only. When Friesz limped back to Paris, he read the papers and discovered that there had been, at precisely the hour of his showing, a total eclipse of the sun.

The Académie Scandinav was run, probably with endless daily headaches, by a very pleasant middle-aged Scandinavian woman who bore no resemblance to Garbo, the totally dominating Scandinavian beauty of our time.

Once Braque, whose hands were remarkable for their extraordinary beauty, told us that the only reason that our teachers bothered to come to instruct us on Friday mornings was because older French artists had been willing to criticize them when they were young.

Jeanne Daour, a student at the Académie Scandinav, took me around to Brancusi's studio one afternoon. He was cordial to her, a fellow Rumanian, and was obviously a resonant and warm man. The light in the studio was what all of us young artists longed for.

He sat on the edge of a bathtub—the dirtiest bathtub I'd ever seen—smoking a pipe in the delicate blue afternoon light. (I later learned that he used this tub for developing his meticulous photographs.) After a long silence while we absorbed the works in progress, he opined, "Love everything, accept everything, and don't try too hard." With those tablets carved upon our skulls we departed, feeling heightened from merely being near this great man. As I aged, I realized that about sixty percent of his statements were pure bathos, yet when we were young and floundering, they seemed to help.

Our encounter with Picasso was of a different nature. One day, when several of us students were lined up at Foinet's wooden counter with our few francs in hand to buy one tube each of Blockx oil paint, Picasso pulled up in front of the store in a landaulet Hispano-Suiza, with Olga Picasso sitting stiffly in the enclosed rear. Picasso was riding exposed to the weather with the uniformed chauffeur. Dismounting like some minor windstorm, blustering into Foinet's, and simply shoving us aside with both arms, he pointed to ten of this, twenty of that, three of that, and forty zinc whites—all Blockx. Gentle M. Foinet calmly collected them, an assistant wrapped them, and Picasso thundered out, tossed them in the rear with Olga, strode around to the left of the chauffeur, bent the door handle down, leapt in, and the whole strange production was gone. We slowly formed up again, our francs in hand; for Blockx's cerulean blue mixed with his whites gave a great deal to any young painter. This was true also of his Naples yellow.

* * *

I gave my grandfather Wyckoff's Gemünder violin to Jeanne Daour. She had studied with Enesco in Budapest and was playing well on a violin that looked like painted orange tin. The two of us used to go to the Salle Pleyel on free passes from Enesco to watch that inexpertly dressed man, his coattails practically tucked inside his descending trousers, play a Bach partita until your own heart bore strings. The two Menuhins sat in a

Picasso

Georges Enesco

box ten feet from us and from him, motionless, overcome.

That violin I took to Paris was the one which I had, in desperation, tried to smash one day as I got off the Oshkosh streetcar taking me to my hated Saturday morning lesson at Miss Emily Barber's house. The early charm of her dark eyebrows had soon worn off as she began to wrench and then bend my left hand around the violin's neck until I stopped the G string to her satisfaction. But it was I who had begged for violin lessons in the first place, to counterbalance Chandler's studying the piano. I failed to observe that he was already shedding tears on the keys as he struggled dutifully to prepare for his next Saturday morning lesson with Clarence Sheperd who had studied with Dupré, the French organist, but who couldn't resist twisting Chandler's hair at every incorrect note.

PARIS—CASSIS

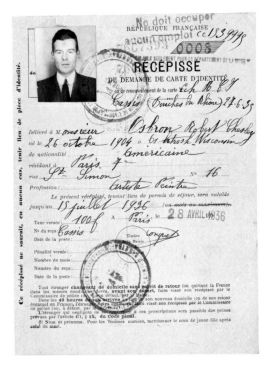

Carte d'identité

In the summer of 1935 I went to the small village of Cassis on the Mediterranean. It was there that I first encountered the stupendous stupidities of bureaucracy. Planning to stay for four months, I secured a Cassis *carte d'identité* in the mayor's tiny office.

In the fall, when I took the train back to Paris, I had to transfer the card from Cassis to Paris. At the enormous Paris municipal hall I waited an entire morning, inching along a bench, and was eventually assigned to a little old woman in a black smock. She gave me the necessary papers and told me to come back when I had filled them out, also to bring fifty *centimes* worth of stamps, which I could buy at any tobacconist's. She would then get in touch with Cassis and notify me when to appear again—which turned out to be a month later because Cassis could find no record of my having been there. Another morning blown. I showed her my Cassis *carte*. She examined it closely and with suspicion, took down a long number, and told me she would notify me.

Three months passed. At last I was told to report. More bench-inching until I reached her counter. She had aged somewhat; the black smock had turned an ashen grey; the protective cardboard cuffs were now frayed and greasy. But when she saw me her eyes sparkled as she held up the new Parisian *carte d'identité*. I looked at it. We both smiled. She said, "Thirty-three francs." To which I replied, "But Madame, I am leaving for Cassis this afternoon."

A terrible anger suffused her face and her whole tiny frame stiffened. She seized the *carte*, tore it to pieces, flung it back over her right shoulder, and screamed, "*Futez le camp!*"

* * *

One summer morning in Cassis I suggested to fawnlike Evelyn Cazalis that we go to a nearby yet lonely *calanque*. After changing at the steep shore's edge, I dove into the clear, deep water and swam about a bit, but when

I tried to return to the sloping rock, I sensed that some force was dragging me out toward deeper water. I attempted to swim in again and realized that I was in serious trouble. I shouted to young Evelyn, "*Cherchez un filin, vite, cherchez un filin!*" To which, jumping about on the rocks and clapping her hands, she screamed back, "*Oui! c'est joli! . . . Oui! c'est joli!*"

Suddenly I knew that I might drown and, becoming totally cunning, as a wounded animal becomes incredibly cunning, I waited for a smaller incoming wave, said to myself, "Okay, *this* is it!" and on its thrust I applied my last strength, made it to the sloping rock's edge, and was out of the water before the next pounding wave struck. In the beautiful, slanting afternoon light, we walked back to Cassis and I dropped Evelyn off at her parents' front door, wiser.

Years later, along the eastern shoreline of Martha's Vineyard, I was always extremely careful of the slightest feel of tugging that could draw me or our sons relentlessly to sea. It is difficult under those circumstances to remain calm and floating; to allow yourself to be carried well out before being circulated back down or up the coast to an achievable shore. Ben Shahn lost his brother off the Cape because he fought against the tow and finally drowned.

In Paris I pursued Jerome Hill's sister, getting nowhere. Maude was deeply in love with the captain, no less, of the Stanford University football team. He was described as very brawny and was, I felt when I later met him, pretentious. She had been taken away from him by her mother, along with a nice cousin, Georgiana Slade, to spend a year abroad. Maude used to play a Weiner and Doucet two-piano record of Jerome Kern's "Along came Bill . . . who's not the type at all . . ." etc., until we *all* got the message.

The next summer Mrs. Hill, Jerome, Corty Hill, Maude, Jack Barrett, and I lived at the Hôtel Beau Site, looking out on the Etoile. There were excellent meals, a great deal of tennis at the tennis club in the Bois, and tangoing afternoons at the Pré Catalan.

One day we five, *sans* Mrs. Hill, set forth in an open maroon Bugatti to drive to the Cap d'Antibes and the

All of us in the Hills' first Bugatti

Cassis-sur-Mer

Hotel Eden Roc. There we painted fake Derains, played tennis on the court next to the luxuriating Dolly sisters, swam a great deal, and dined very well under a great awning beside the Mediterranean in a temperature which seemed to be part of the food.

I recount this spoiled behavior to present honestly our slow, unaware development in a period when this sort of life was not only acceptable, it was desired.

*   *   *

Every year that I was in Paris, I spent a lot of time and little money at the Cirque Médrano.

There one could see the three Fratellinis, their unbelievable visual wit as essential to their broad humor as it was to their slightest petallike comic touches. Most important, they collectively possessed comic imagination such as I had never encountered. Grock you can have; Emmet Kelly seemed very limited, subtle as he was; Popov had a wonderful, broad Russian slam to him; but in my lifetime it was the Fratellinis live. Of course, on film it was Keaton and, above all, Chaplin.

One afternoon at the *cirque* I saw one Fratellini—the golden clown in the classic pointed cap, high shoulders, and white ballet stockings ending in tight golden slippers—come out quietly, alone, moved by the spotlight to the exact center of the broad stage. He was twirling a ten-inch weight on a very short, almost invisible rope. He did it very nonchalantly, but the line imperceptibly increased in length at every movement of his arm and wrist as the weight began to fly around him, the pivot.

A chimney sweep in a tall black hat strolled into the possible circle with his equipment and took his position seven feet from the golden clown. Then came two carpenters with a short board, a doctor with his case, the red-wigged male Fratellini in a female nurse's costume. Three feet farther out, a tourist photographer strolled, and six feet beyond him, a plasterer with his trowel and pail.

By this time the act had set its clear form. The golden clown at the center was still swinging the thin rope—which began to look like a ring around the planet Saturn—feeding out line until the lethal weight was

Two views of Maude Hill

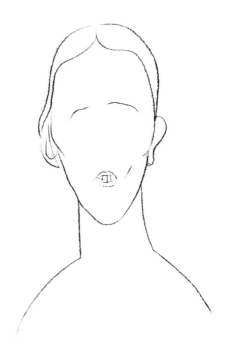

whizzing around the ring at neck height of all the characters. As it came to each person, he would neatly dip his knees, it would fly by, and they would resume sawing, or talking, or whatever, until in a few seconds the line and weight came sizzling by again. Then one sensed that just as the weight had moved out, it was now being imperceptibly returned to the twirling golden wrist. No longer endangered, the other actors finished their tasks or talk and departed the ring one by one, until only the golden clown was left at its center, gently twirling the heavy, yellow, zucchinilike weight on the vanished line. Standing alone, with a discreet smile on his paste-white face, he pocketed the weight in his full pantaloons, bowed in four directions to the screaming audience, and departed from the central ring.

I could not believe what I had seen. I rushed back to 16 rue St. Simon to alert and gather painter friends for the evening performance. I didn't quite promise total salvation, but almost. We all sat in the upper rows and the three Fratellinis and their dog presented an entirely different, completely undistinguished program. I limped home early.

*   *   *

As the money earned at Yale began to run out, I wrote to the headmaster at Hotchkiss asking if he still wanted me to come and start an art department. No answer. Each day I went to the Morgan Bank on the Place Vendôme to ask if a cable had come for Robert Osborn. *Rien!* By then I was down to $150—barely a boat passage home. At last, on an August noon, it arrived. I didn't open it at once, walking instead to a place behind the Orangerie and beneath a stone statue of a faun. There, I cooked up my courage, tore open the envelope and read: *Do come. Job still open. We would like to have you here. George Van Santvoord.*

In view of my financial predicament, it was good news. I bought a boat passage at American Express, packed my steamer trunk, and happily set out for Connecticut to teach Art with a capital A. That was in the fall of 1929.

HOTCHKISS

Hotchkiss is a fine preparatory school set upon a hill in Lakeville, Connecticut. It looks out over a handsome Berkshire landscape complete with a perfectly scaled lake.

I was given a room on the top floor of the headmaster's house. The only fault with that was that he enjoyed talking until one or two in the morning. He was very erudite but couldn't resist showing it. Under his direction, however, the intellectual standards of the entire school were clearly being heightened.

My tasks were to coach football in the fall, track in the spring, manage the trap and skeet teams, teach the history of art, and, best of all, to conduct a rapidly changing series of pictures and ideas on a north wall of the long main corridor which all students passed each day. I had brought plenty of color prints of paintings back from Europe, and began with whole shows of my favorite, Cézanne. No boys stopped to stare. I switched to Degas and still no students really looked. I was finally forced to show the aesthetics of a plane's propeller, a Bugatti car design, a Bauhaus building. I even used cartoons I drew to engage their attention. It was then possible to slowly lead them back toward a Rembrandt, a Mondrian, a Seurat.

One young painter I influenced (his words) was William Kienbusch. There was another truly endowed young sculptor, named Rossbach, whose facility astonished me. These two and others worked in the low-ceilinged basement of the headmaster's house. We painted it white, installed a wood-burning stove, and there we all felt, at least during those pleasant hours, that we were free of the school's rigid requirements.

Considering those times, simply having a job, being warm, and having food and $1200 a year during the worst of the Depression was a rare situation.

One day I was to take the Hotchkiss painting class of six to a deserted, handsome hillside with a magnificent

Coaching skeet shooting at Hotchkiss

view north from Taconic. Orson Welles and John Hoysradt (Hotchkiss '22) showed up just as we were setting off. Two extra shoebox luncheons were supplied at the last minute by the commissary, no questions asked.

There, on that fine site, we all labored, to very little avail. Orson drew pretty well; Kienbusch drew better than any of us. As we all gazed out and drew what we saw, Orson, who had produced Shakespeare at age seventeen, suddenly began to speak in that language. He spoke first as he sat. Then, dropping the pencil and the paper and slowly rising cobralike to his knees, gestures starting, his voice rising and deepening in measured cadence, now the legs fully unbent, he began to deliver Hamlet's skull speech with hill-shaking resonance—his arms and hands encompassing the whole valley and the mountains beyond, his entire body trembling.

My young charges, huddled on the grass about him, had never seen anything like this. It was a dumbfounding, mesmerizing performance and we were all lucky to have been there to have seen it.

Welles was a genius—fullblown, self-destructive, overly endowed. I think of him in the rich image of Falstaff, my favorite Shakespearean character, as presented by Welles in his under-budgeted movie *Chimes at Midnight,* with the most terrifying battle-slaughtering sequences of man by man I have ever seen.

* * *

It was while I was teaching at Hotchkiss that I asked Mary Rheinhart of the Rheinhart Gallery in New York if I could bring down some of my recent paintings for a criticism. Our mothers had known each other in Wisconsin and she had known Chandler at the University of Wisconsin. She kindly agreed and I brought down a large wicker hamper, loaded with oils. I showed them to her one by one in the brown velvet-covered room.

First she asked, "Do you want a frank critique?"

"Oh yes," I replied, opening the hamper and triumphantly bringing out a picture of violets.

She looked for a moment and then said, "But didn't Manet do those violets better?"

Next.

"But hasn't Renoir painted those very pears?"

Sketching Orson Welles that very day

Some of the corridor
pictures used at Hotchkiss

Still assured, I went on showing her my imitation Manets, Renoirs, Cézannes—all knowledgeable paintings but devoid of any exploration on my part. None of her criticism was meanly said; she was trying to help.

I packed the hamper, thanked her, and caught the 4:32 Harlem Division "rattler" back to Millerton. It took about eight months to recover from the truth. Like a dumb boxer absorbing blows to the jaws, which take away their hinges and his hearing, I began again, this time producing imitative Roger de la Fresnayes, blind to the fact that they were equally devitalized.

Two years after I had failed to face Mary Rheinhart's correct estimations—still wading in, head down, flailing away in anything but an aware fashion—I asked Duncan MacDonald at the Bignou Gallery, where they showed the very best Cézannes, if I could bring in my latest paintings. He flattered me politely but also pointed out what I was actually doing.

*   *   *

The first Hotchkiss year was pure pleasure, except for my not being able to tell the headmaster that I was tired of his remarkable erudition and that I had a class to prepare for and teach at eight-thirty the next morning. The afternoon athletic life was good and kept me in shape. With George Milmine, who had loaned me twenty dollars until my first paycheck arrived, I coached a secondary football team, planning elaborate plays during tea at the end of the afternoon. Too, with him, I would go to Saturday luncheons or skating parties given by Orlena Scoville, who lived nearby. They were welcome relief from being with younger minds. She was a very attractive woman, older than I.

The second year was equally enjoyable, the third as well, and by then I was teaching effectively, even though the Greek philosophy course that I had to give once a week with Van Santvoord remained something of a trial.

I spent my first lengthy summer vacation, in 1930, with my parents, who were having a poor time because the Depression had actually begun in the lumber industry two years before it engulfed the nation. In Wisconsin I painted steadily but still without originality. I had a shell on the Fox River and rowed in the evening for exercise; I

George Milmine and I lunching
at the Scovilles'

66

also read a great deal.

The summer of 1931 I returned to Paris and again went to Cassis-sur-Mer to paint and to swim. There, at the Hotel Roches Blanches, I met Ophélia de Rougé, a French viscountess—actually, a Brazilian married to a French viscount. She wrote poetry, was a good friend of Paul Valéry, and had a Russian friend named Lily Pastré—obviously rich—who owned a large villa just east of Marseilles. The place was crawling with bored, cynical, lazy White Russian indigents. Ophélia, on the other hand, swam a lot, enjoyed music—Mozart and Brahms in particular—and concentrated on her poetry. She was also older than I and became a helpful, liberating, and close friend.

For the summer of 1933 I went to Salzburg with the Daniels family of Minneapolis. I was to tutor the two bright sons, which was easily done, and the summer's greatest pleasure was naturally the music.

We all heard Richard Strauss conduct his ranging music, saw—at close quarters—Bruno Walter conduct Mozart from a harpsichord in the Mozarteum, and often enough Toscanini came to lend his Italian magic. This went on all summer long. Max Reinhardt was also there, using up Tilly Losch's talents producing *Jedermann*.

At the west edge of Salzburg, beside and a bit above the river, there was a monastery which brewed a beer that ought to have convinced Schlitz and Miller to give up. The monks served it beneath spreading plane trees on a terrace overlooking the river. Sherman Kent, a friend from Yale, arrived in Salzburg for a day or so and I suggested that we go there. As the afternoon drew to a close while we sat drinking on the increasingly boisterous terrace, I noticed that Sherman was gazing directly into the sun without even blinking. We wobbled back into town on our rented bicycles.

I painted a portrait of Frances Daniels, an imitative Savely Sorine effort, but the presentation of her character was honest even though I could not control the picture's tone, which became too warm, too russet.

At the end of the summer I took the two sons to Vienna and showed them that delightful city. We stayed at Sachers Hotel for six dollars a day each, complete. The waiters' elbows were threadbare and there was no one

Ophélia de Rougé

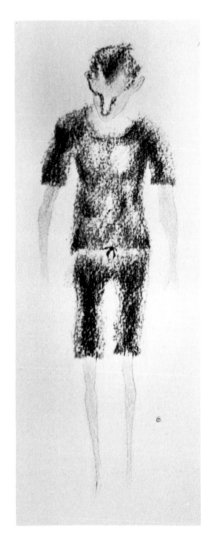

The rented bathing suit

else in the dining room. We walked down to the Danube, bought three tickets, boarded a river boat, and rode gently all day toward Budapest, where we saw one of the truly great Vermeers.

At the zoo I looked at the tiger pacing in its cage and thought that I understood the movement of the beast and its shoulders. Once outside, I sensed that perhaps I didn't, so I paid the small admission and returned to stare for another half hour, trying to comprehend the rhythm of the legs and pads being placed, denied the jungle.

The women of any age in Hungary are beautiful. As one passes them in the streets the eyes and, even better, the clear, strong, high cheekbones, are unlike any others we see.

At the electric-wave pool across the Danube from Buda, I saw a very handsome young girl. Using those false waves, I managed to meet her. The sad fact was that I was in a long-sleeved, long-legged, black cotton rented bathing suit and her male friend, who promptly joined us, was barely clothed. I made a drawing of her later to fix my memory.

* * *

At the end of three revealing months, the Daniels and I left by one of those glorious trains, crossed the cultivated landscapes to Cherbourg, and there caught a liner to New York. In the twenties and thirties travel was still entirely pleasurable in itself—the service, the surroundings, the cleanliness, the food, the linen. . . . And the steamers and trains worked.

* * *

By the time I was half-way into the fifth year at Hotchkiss, the enchantment of being in that school, even in the Berkshire hills, was gone; and because of the various psychological strains, emotional denials, and the over-intellectualized life, the ancient duodenal ulcer perforated one Sunday morning after I had eaten, of all things, some kippered herring. The school doctor, Harry Wieler, saved me by his unstinting care and by getting a prompt diagnosis of the excruciating pain as well as the right surgeon to perform what was called a purse-string suture.

Four days after the operation, the headmaster appeared at my bedside and, despite two draining tubes in my nostrils, wanted to know what I thought the next Greek philosophy assignment should be.

Some ten days later, Orlena Scoville wrote to ask if I would like to recuperate at Hill House. She would be in Portugal starting work on the restoration of the Quinta da Bacalhôa in Azeitão but the servants would be in Taconic and could care for me.

Of course I more than welcomed that kindness and I spent the spring there, drawing and doing watercolors.

Marion Willard, who ran an art gallery, used to come up from New York and, along with her friend Toni Hughes, tried to show me my failures and to redirect my life. But it was Nancy Wilson Ross, the writer, who was of even more help—for she was very gentle in her suggestions and entirely feminine in her approach. Thanks to all of these friends, I began reading Jung.

Because I had told Van Santvoord that I would not be back in the fall of 1935, it seemed wise to apply for a Prix de Rome. I painted a standing male nude and a required "composition" using sketches and paintings of various swimmers surrounding a Cassis sailboat. I submitted photographs of them and never heard another word.

Undaunted (and my determination to be a "great" artist was unduly dogged), I gathered up my belongings and, even before the Depression had clearly ended, left Hotchkiss knowing that it was too compressive, too correct—no standing on the table, no shouting, ever, and that admired headmaster inhibiting everything.

Having saved $1300, and having sold my third-hand jalopy for $35, I set off once again for beloved France.

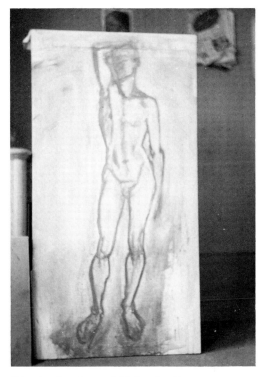

Start of rejected Prix de Rome painting

BACK TO EUROPE

At the end of that winter in Paris, I boarded a train and went down to Cintra, Portugal, in the early spring of 1936 to get some sun and to meet Orlena.

At Cintra, W. H. Auden, Christopher Isherwood, Stephen Spender, and a beautiful young German boy were all living together. When they came to lunch at the Nûnes Hotel they made very lively conversation. Auden was aware of Freud and was flinging his concepts about at the drop of a hat, even to why I had a head cold. We met them all through an English woman, Mary Norton, who later wrote *The Borrowers*, which luckily provided her with some money. Her overbearing, half-Portuguese, half-English husband was trying to make a living quick-freezing sardines when salting sardines was perfectly adequate. He reminded me a great deal of Mr. Radford in Oshkosh.

Leaving Cintra, Orlena and I drove through Spain in fine weather to enjoy, as we knew we would, all of the pleasures of Spain at Easter. On that trip El Greco impressed me most, his sensitivity and painterly qualities. How Velásquez's great talent could have escaped me I don't know, or Goya's! Later both were to replace El Greco, though he certainly remains a remarkable painter.

We parted at Gilbraltar; she left for America, and I boarded a small, antique steamer to Marseilles and from there to Cassis, for another summer of drawing, painting, and working on a movie Jerome Hill was to shoot there. He and Jeanne Daour and Ophélia came down from Paris and stayed at the Roches Blanches, Jerome supporting talented, complicated Jeanne. I found a cheap turquoise-blue room over the small bar at the west end of the handsome quay. Each morning I would have coffee there in the early light of summer. Often Varda, a Greek painter, would join me and tell stories of pure fantasy. He had with him a stunning Dutch girl, but as the summer wore on she switched to Jerome.

Doing the movie was more than interesting. We were all amateurs and consequently learned a great deal when the rushes came back from Paris. Knowing no rules we were able to do things which we had not seen done or even experimented with, certainly not in Hollywood. As you can imagine, those summers in that still small and simple Mediterranean fishing port were memorable. Before we all left for Paris I took Jeanne Daour up to Fuveau, which we thought was Cézanne's Gardanne, to do landscapes. She had no *carte d'identité* so we slept out in fields to avoid the inquiring police. We soon moved on to Avignon and from across the river we sketched and painted the Pope's Palace, that most satisfactory pile of white stone which turns to pink in the late afternoon.

Back in Paris I lived at 16 rue St. Simon, worked there all day, and then drew at La Grande Chaumière from five to seven, at least learning more of the complexities of the human figure and its articulation. Trying as it was, it was well worth it. Young artists drawing today, some for the *New Yorker,* must feel scanted by not having the clear bone-to-bone, muscle-binding anatomical knowledge that Matisse, Miró, and Picasso had by the time they were seventeen. Without it, a great deal of comprehension, conviction, and the convincing lines are lost to the artist, especially to the drawer. George Price, on the contrary, understands these things so well that he can leave out whole passages and still have firmly articulated figures, lamps, detritus, faces. Matisse, of course, after years of the most careful study could, in the second half of his life, discard lines and distill figures until they were entirely transmuted, yet pulsing with life. I think too of the blue cut-out bathers at the very end.

Avignon from across the river

RETURN TO THE UNITED STATES

On the room's fire escape

By the fall of 1937 I was astonished to discover that I was beginning to long for America, even for the black soil of Wisconsin. Respecting these feelings, I set forth for New York in tourist class on the S.S. *Bremen*, which at one point looked as though it would break apart amidship in a frightening storm on truly mountainous seas.

In New York I looked for a room with a paintable view. I was going to do the definitive oil of New York City!

I found a three-room, cold-water flat with a splendid view down the East River, for seventeen dollars a month. I bought a small stove and carried in coal which I kept on the floor in the painting room; a bed cost three dollars and a mattress four. For three months I painted on a large vertical canvas and several small oils depicting the view south along the river, with the towering white medical center and at its base a handsome brickyard and a brick chimney in which a begger lived. Each morning he would emerge from a hole in the chimney, build a small fire in the fallen brickyard, and move about like an animal in the warming morning sun. Then he'd depart to scrounge for food, returning at dusk to climb through the hole and be gone for the night.

When spring came, Lux Feininger—who lived two blocks north and was painting small ship pictures with very Germanic black skies and a Dürer-like thoroughness—would come down to sit on my small fire escape and talk great theories of art. We two knew!

* * *

But I really don't enjoy cities the way I enjoy being in the country.

The cities—London, Paris, Rome, Budapest, and certainly New York—are always highly stimulating and I take endless pleasure in walking upstream through the torrent of faces on any street in any large city. In New York I can often spend an afternoon looking sharply at the infinite variety of physiognomies, seeing there the miseries, and oftentimes the courage, while others look like pleasure-seeking wind-up toys.

The welcome summer exodus from New York took me to Salisbury, Connecticut, where Emerson Quaile offered me the top floor of a Salisbury School dormitory. He was its headmaster and a generous man. We had shot together in earlier days.

Evenings often included summer dinner parties on the Scovilles' stone terrace. The view was spectacular, and still is. Looking northward one could frequently see Greylock Mountain, forty miles away across the Poussin-like landscape.

* * *

During the fall of 1938 I went to Wisconsin to be with mother and father. On January 15, 1939, after having made many small studies in Oshkosh, I left for Azeitão to do a nine-by-eight-foot mural for the large entrance hall of the Quinta da Bacalhôa, the Scovilles' house, purchased in 1934 in a nearly ruined state.

The building itself, as a private dwelling, I can only compare to the Villa Lante in Italy. Villa Lante is more exquisitely ordered, yet Bacalhôa has a riveting, provincial force to it that the Villa Lante lacks.

I worked on the painting for nearly eight months, with those helpful Blockx colors that M. Foinet would send down from Paris. It was a good period. Life there was direct and certainly enjoyable.

Suddenly, the squalid Munich performance took place and all Americans were ordered home.

I had finished the picture and was pleased at last by the sense of the slow movement of the cape, the matador's leading arm, his entire stance, the exact tilt of his head beneath the raised, encrusted shoulder. I saw the painting once later, after Orlena Scoville had died, and I still liked these things. In no other picture—not even in all of the sure and marvelous Goyas—have I seen to my satisfaction that slow, majestic movement of the cape, barely sustained before the sharp and hooking horn.

Once I had watched Belmonte's son bring an unbelievable slowness to that union of the man and bull and cape. I can still recall that afternoon and the ring. Later, as the wars increased, killing purely for excitement be-

View south at the end of 72nd Street

Mural for Quinta da Bacalhôa

came repulsive, and I wondered why it had interested me in the first place.

* * *

Back in Connecticut I acquired a small white farmhouse north of Taconic. It was valued at two thousand dollars. I moved in on February 15, 1940, after having lived at the White Hart Inn for a month painting an oil portrait of Orlena. It was honest and seemed solid and looked like an "Osborn."

On taking over the house, which was heated by one downstairs Franklin stove, I painted all the walls white and proceeded to a series of winter landscapes.

The course of my life was clearly visible in the pictures I was turning out, although I didn't see this at the time. I was working very hard but the results were anything but breathtaking. Actually, I was slowly coming apart within. The paintings, which I was then doing on solid wood panels, were becoming smaller and smaller and I sensed that my intellectualized life was becoming less and less satisfying. In desperation, I wrote to Carl Jung in Zurich asking one question, hoping for an answer. In return I offered him a thick book on tribal practices that Sumner and Keller of Yale had assembled. I felt sure that the book would be helpful to him at that point in his pursuits. I hoped that his words would be helpful to me.

Back came a two-page, single-spaced reply which was discreet beyond belief. In it Jung suggested that if I took one course or another I might encounter certain unwished-for results. His words and ideas were very subtly chosen. He laid down no hard and fast rules, and he left all possibilities open to choice, yet I knew at once what I could and could not do.

I wrote him promptly to thank him for his advice and sent the promised volume. He wrote back two shorter, cordial and relaxed letters offering one more piece of gentle advice and thanking me for the casebook. I could see that it had had meaning for him and was of use. What a lucky exchange.

Another piece of lucky timing was my doing three cartoon books: *How to Shoot Ducks*, *How to Shoot Quail*, and *How to Catch Trout*. Tim Coward of Coward

The first three cartoon books

Orlena Scoville

McCann asked for them, and the first Christmas they sold forty thousand copies. When the royalty checks began to arrive I could not believe what had happened. I was certainly being told what I should be doing.

But the most sustaining part of my life was the relationship with Orlena Scoville. The other older woman, the French viscountess Ophélia de Rougé, gave me much in a short time after we met in Cassis, but I am sure that without the help of Orlena I might have failed completely—she was that important to me at that crucial point. An intelligent, inquiring human being, she chose to believe in my ability and perceptions at a time when there was very little to go on. I am infinitely grateful to her and count it a great pity that she did not, before her death, see what she had given to me and what I gained from it.

WORLD WAR II AND THE NAVY

Before America got into World War II, I tried to join the Canadian Royal Air Force. I was turned down when I told them about the ulcer. They said that I could serve as a "bat boy" for a young able-bodied pilot. I was thirty-seven at the time. They also suggested that I go back to Connecticut and raise tomatoes, can them, and send them to London, because tomatoes contain drinkable water and essential vitamins. Some thirty Salisbury townspeople raised and canned fourteen tons of tomatoes, which reached London despite the submarines, as the Lord Mayor's letter to all of us attested.

There were many Americans who sensed early on that Hitler and the Nazi attack was truly dangerous and had to be stopped. There were others, like Lindbergh and his wife, who should have known better, but simply didn't seem to comprehend the enormous threat to all civilized values.

I had seen Hitler back in 1935. Two Austrian maid-servants in the *schloss* where I was working as a tutor asked me to go with them to hear Herr Hitler. We rode eight miles on our bicycles to a gigantic prepared field. There, with great fanfares, he finally, dramatically, appeared. As he began to speak, then shout, the entire plain seemed charged with a terrible vindictive, then hating, then glorifying emotion. I couldn't believe what I was hearing and seeing, but the two young Austrian girls were still crying as we pulled into the gate after our long ride home.

America didn't seem to comprehend that between World War I and World War II our fortunes and our future had become inextricably connected to the rest of the world and especially western Europe. However, the instant the Japanese attacked us and FDR came on the radio that Sunday morning, the determination and, more important, the productive vitality of our country was unleashed.

*   *   *

Finally, canned tomatoes

On December 8, 1941, I tried to enlist in the Navy at the local post office in Connecticut. I preferred the cleaner sea to the pounded land. I was told to go to New Haven. In New Haven I was told to go to Poughkeepsie and from there I was told to go to 90 Church Street in New York City.

By that time, I was becoming less belligerent by the day, but thanks to the two Agar brothers, Herbert and William, whom I knew in Taconic, I was sent to the Navy Department in Washington with a letter to an old friend of theirs in Naval Aviation. He, in turn, very perceptively sent me to see a brilliant Naval Reserve captain, Louis de Florez, and also to a flight training section. There I met Captain Arthur Radford and, better than Radford, a feisty Commander A. K. Doyle. They were both sitting on boards resting on pulled-out middle drawers of their decrepit desks. Such was the state of our preparedness.

I showed Doyle the three shooting and fishing books I'd drawn the year before, and which the Agars had suggested I bring along, and he at once got papers started for my enlistment, despite the still persistent duodenal ulcer. This all took place, I am sure, because these regular Navy officers had seen how the British Royal Air Force had been bright and traditionally lighthearted enough to produce training manuals using cartoons.

I went back to Connecticut to wait for orders. Finally, a month later, I was told to go to Floyd Bennett Field. There, a suspicious and most unpleasant lieutenant commander said, "And what is this *miracle* you are going to work for the Navy?" I mumbled something about having been "requested" by Radford and Doyle, and departed to order uniforms at Brooks Brothers. I was even expected to buy a sword, a fancy belt, and a scabbard.

I bid the white walls of my small farmhouse good-bye, closed the rooms where I had struggled so hard to be a "painter," and left by the Harlem Division train for the Navy Department in Washington.

The Navy was very perceptive in its use of me. I was assigned to a unit that produced Sense Books, a series of lively pamphlets with text and cartoons covering all manner of flying hazards. In particular, I devised a car-

Steichen's photograph of me

toon character named Dilbert, a dumb but cheerful cadet pilot whose mistakes were a constant menace. Before I was through I drew some two thousand Dilbert posters about how *not* to fly, how to prepare and care for planes, and how to avoid accidents and death. In the process I must have drawn over thirty thousand sketches, studies, printable drawings, and color overlays. I came out of the Navy able to draw a perfect circle, with my eyes closed, any hour of the day or night.

The writers, such as Robert Lewis Taylor and Roarke Bradford, and I would be sent out to naval air stations or to the Pacific to study the problems, write texts that were lighthearted but factual, and, in my case, produce the pictures.

I learned to fly in yellow Stearman biplanes at the Atlanta Naval Air Station. I was worse than Dilbert. Then on to more advanced training, flying by day and drawing in the late afternoon and evening.

The posters and the Sense Books were printed in enormous editions by the Navy printing office. At the start of the war there were seven of us in the Training Literature Unit, including our perceptive and encouraging commander, "Min" Miller. At the end of the war, and probably producing less because of the adhesions of red tape, there were a hundred and ten officers in the unit.

Because the German submarines along the east coast were menacing and because planes were being thrown into that frantic battle, I had to go out on U.S. submarines in the Atlantic to see what these boats were like, how they behaved, and where they were vulnerable. We would be attacked by U.S. Navy torpedo bombers, Grumman TBFs mostly, and would then dive to "escape." Being five hundred feet under water made me very queasy, and I was glad to get back on dry land and to be drawing what I'd learned.

Then for several days I would fly in the attacking bombers. I'm six feet one and squeezing myself up into the tail gunner's capsule was a trial. If anything had gone wrong in flight I'm sure I would never have extricated myself, with a chute, in time.

Still, I enjoyed making the drawings—about two hundred in that antisubmarine set—and I was told later that they were a distinct help. Actually it was the Allied

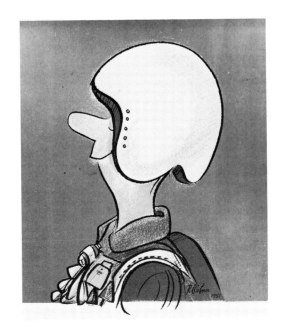

Dilbert

The U.S. Navy printed, in various forms, over 18,000 ideas

Navy pilots and the many small, rapidly built carriers that halted the decimating attacks of the German undersea boats which, at one point, were strangling England. Churchill later admitted that they were his greatest concern.

RAF pilots have told me that during the North African campaign against Rommel, the English found batches of our Dilbert posters at the captured German airfields, reprinted in Germany and recaptioned in German.

*   *   *

I was fortunate in that my desk was next to Edward Steichen's all through the war. It was particularly ironic that this outstanding American photographer, who had pioneered the use of aerial photography for the U.S. Army during World War I, was turned down by the U.S. Air Force in World War II when he once again promptly volunteered for military service. The Navy, given a chance to recruit him, wisely did so. Steichen in turn enlisted the best photographers he knew for his unit.

One of the more pleasant aspects of the war were the conversations the two of us would have when everyone

U.S. NAVY

Intrepid Steichen in the Pacific

Just married

else had left after the day's labor. We would sit there in the failing light talking of such things as Wisconsin, France, Rodin, early photography, his first delphinium experiments just north of Paris, how the Germans had overrun his garden in World War I, and how they had now done it for the second time, with their usual arrogance, coarseness, and brutality.

Steichen was an intrepid man. Although well on in years, he went out to the battle zones and took some of the finest photographs produced by the special photographic section he captained.

Some months after arriving in Washington I met Elodie Courter. She ran a department at the Museum of Modern Art and had come to discuss with Steichen a traveling show of Navy photographs taken by his remarkable unit. She came through the door on the third floor of the old Navy Building. My desk was six feet from Steichen's and as I looked up there she was. Steichen rose and welcomed her. I thought she looked either French or Belgian.

Steichen pointed to me and said, "Now there is an artist who is really doing something for the war effort, instead of those painters you are showing at the museum." Generous, but wide of the mark.

When Elodie and Steichen finished, he seemed to push us together. I led her around the room pointing out Atget qualities in this photograph, Bresson qualities in another, trying to indicate to this very attractive young woman that I was not a dolt; that I knew about art! When she left I took her to our office door and told her how to get to the staircase, suggesting lunch the next time she came down.

There followed a great deal of letter-writing back and forth, a number of meetings in Washington, and a year later, after a drawing assignment that took me to New York for two months, we were married—just before I was sent to the Pacific.

On the U.S.S. *Essex* I worked on what was to be my last assignment. I saw the whole Saipan and Iwo Jima battles, with those unthinking Japanese pilots boring in toward their premeditated deaths. I met my brother, Chandler, who was on another carrier, and I saw the

At sea with Chandler

American fleet, by then so enormous and swiftly built that as one came on deck for the dawn watch American ships stretched across the entire curvature of the horizon.

*   *   *

The pilot who had taught me to fly at the Atlanta Naval Air Station appeared in a squadron of fighters on the *Essex*. During the battle for Saipan his plane was hit and he was seriously wounded. He managed to be guided back some eighty miles to the carrier, blood streaming down his face, his sight failing, two wing men telling him what to do. From below it became increasingly apparent that he was not going to make it down, and that if he did come in wildly and out of control he would certainly crash into needed planes. As we all watched, he simply flew away, leaving the task force and his friends continuing on into the dusk of that alien sea. I cannot resolve this image in my mind even today: the view of a young man departing to death.

About the time that the bomb was delivered to Tinian, an island I had been sent to, my duodenal ulcer finally seized up and I flew home in the cold tail of a PBY, sleeping on mail sacks while four admirals sat up front in the warmer seats. In San Francisco I stayed in a small hotel, in a room with all of the curtains pulled down, for five days until my orders came through to proceed to Washington. There I caught a train to New York to join my wife. She tells me that as I came along East 57th Street to the apartment I was wavering and delirious from serious dehydration. With the help of medical friends, she got me to the St. Albans Naval Hospital in an ambulance and a noted Captain Kreer Ferguson, who ran that hospital, did the resection of my stomach. There has been no pain since.

The Department of Naval Aviation was more than appreciative of what I had contributed to the saving of lives and planes and was very generous in awarding me various honors and medals.

What *I* discovered in the Navy was that I had an ability to quickly comprehend a problem, organize its components, and then produce the drawings that explained what needed to be known. The humor was added to assure attention.

ELODIE

For the different loves of three quite different women, I am deeply grateful. I don't think that I would still be alive save for them.

But it was Elodie Courter who became the true meaning of my life. Nothing that I have done has meant as much in the end as this extraordinary human relationship. She has enhanced the hours and days of the last four decades.

John Cheever once wrote me referring to Elodie as "your astonishingly beautiful wife." Her great-grandmother was Belgian, a lady-in-waiting at the Court. A pastel of her looks very much like Elodie. Against the family's wishes, Elodie's grandmother married a rascal who taught mathematics and astronomy at the University of Leiden, gambled away his wife's inheritance at Monte Carlo, and finally came to America, having been invited to teach at Vassar. He shunned the professorship for the excitement of Wall Street, where he again failed. He caused many fine women a great deal of almost inexhaustible misery.

Elodie

* * *

After I had recovered from the operation I was mustered out of Naval Aviation and Elodie and I went to live at 26 East 63rd Street in New York. Herbert Bayer's wife, Joella, became my agent; we liked both of them. Fairly soon, the drawings began to be sold and we were heartened by the interest shown.

Our son, Nicolas, was conceived and born—a real "force," to quote a friend. When he reached the age where he insisted on picking up everything he could lay his hands on, including cigarette butts during walks in Central Park, I suggested that we try surviving a winter in the tiny Connecticut house.

The five-room house was small, had no indoor toilet, had only a coal stove for heat, but did have a darkroom. Thanks to the plucky, sensitive, considerate, organized, intelligent, funny, delicious woman I married, we had lovely days and nights there. It also finally appeared that various people liked and respected what I was trying to accomplish. From then on I was free to reveal what I felt, draw what I loved—and what I hated.

After the birth of our second son, Eliot, it was clear to Elodie that the demands of a family would make impossible her return to the Museum of Modern Art, from which she had been given a leave of absence. Instead, she helped to bring about a first-class new elementary school in Salisbury, designed by Eliot Noyes. She also started the Salisbury Film Society in 1951 and has run it ever since, showing well over five hundred of the truly distinguished films from all over the world.

Elodie again

Elodie with our sons, Nicolas standing, Eliot asleep on Elodie's lap

NICOLAS COURTER OSBORN
AND
ELIOT WYCKOFF OSBORN

The two sons, Nicolas and Eliot, are both perceptive, honest, articulate, and organized in their own ways. They are full of humor and, above all, kind and thoughtful human beings.

Eliot, from the age of four, had perfect pitch and obviously enjoyed music. One spring day while we were driving to New York, he stood in the back of our small car, barely able to see over the back of the front seat, singing Benjamin Britten's composition for children that

Eliot

reveals what each instrument does in an orchestra. Elodie and I couldn't believe what we were hearing. And when he got to the oboe's musical phrase he suddenly stopped, saying, "No, that's wrong," and going back, started it over again, this time reproducing the sound exactly. We two were practically entangled in the gearshift, truly dumbfounded. Eliot continued blithely on.

Even as a baby Nicolas had strong powers of concentration. For hours on end he would draw, paint, or build large and complex structures with blocks. He has a highly intuitive comprehension of space and of the natural thrusts and forces in water, air, and solids. In white-water racing he and his partner became national champions the second year they competed. Nicolas also has a clearly original filming ability which he evolved entirely on his own. Fitting into the requirements of society is another matter; his strong sense of self sometimes gets in the way.

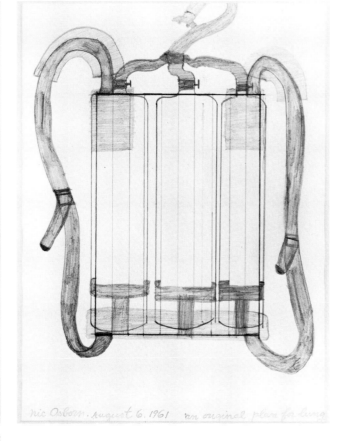

Nicolas

CIVILIAN LIFE

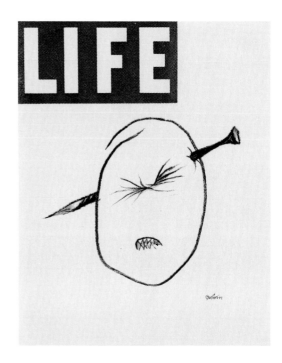

From the very start, when I was twelve, the cartoonist Clare Briggs used ideas I sent him in the *Chicago Tribune*; and he put "+R.O." down in the corner of his drawings. As I mentioned earlier, Harold Ross of the *New Yorker* requested cartoons from me when I was at Yale, as he did from S. J. Perelman at Brown. Then, after the four years of World War II, having finally found my own abilities, the outlets for drawings seemed endless.

Russell Lynes at *Harper's* was the first to print drawings that began to show what I could do. Michael Straight, editing the *New Republic*, was next, and after

Senator Joe McCarthy

Outlets

Straight, Gilbert Harrison also afforded me page after full page on that best of printing paper to put forth the wildest of ideas. Only once during the Joe McCarthy period did they not print one venomous drawing I submitted of that viper. They paid thirty-five or fifty dollars for each drawing used and, to be sure that I was exploring all of the possibilities, I would mail them ten to twenty pictures from which to choose.

The *Atlantic Monthly* also printed large drawings, and at *Life* Charles Tudor initiated the magazine's first *drawn* cover, and even cabled me the news in Paris. The drawing was of a man with a nail going through his head; the article inside was on alcoholism. Sandy Calder later gave me a cut-in-half nail with a wire spring between the two parts. It could be snapped into one ear, and then into the other to demonstrate my drawing. At *Look* Allen

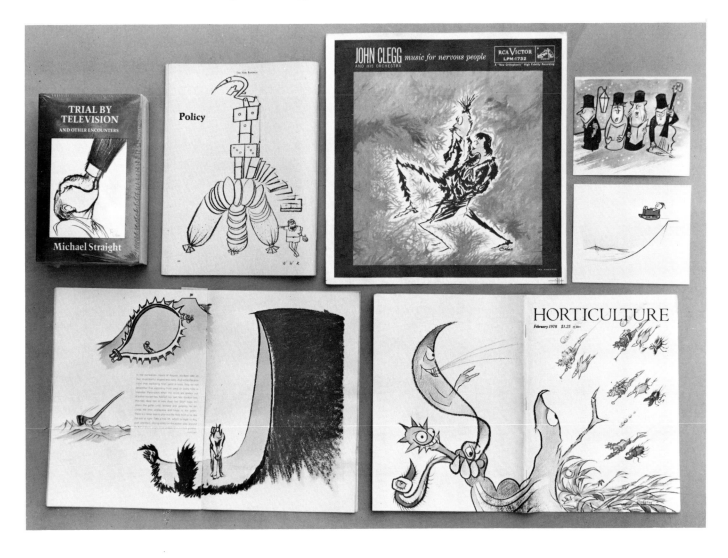

Hurlburt was using my very freest lines and ideas.

There were certain men who were willing to use difficult pictures. Will Burtin at *Fortune* often printed the sketch for an idea rather than the labored-over, "clean" watercolor made for reproduction. Cippi Peneles, Burtin's wife and the art editor for *Mademoiselle*, called for a set of sixteen or seventeen black conté crayon drawings of a man turning into a rhinoceros to illustrate Ionesco's play. Naturally, the fine actor-clown I thought of as I drew the metamorphosis was Zero Mostel.

Edward Thompson, first at *Life* and later the brilliant creator of the *Smithsonian*, called forth my own ideas to illustrate articles he felt I would be interested in.

I am forever grateful for these encouraging and exploring editors.

Progression of an idea

ON ART

That Falstaffian Mr. Gulbenkian said, "Great art makes you feel young and strong and glad." Surely that is true. I once wrote on my studio wall, "Great art is something you can hardly stand."

My favorite contemporary painters are Matisse and Miró. Above them, I place some Cézannes, produced by that extraordinary, searching, beaten-down, incredible giant of our times. Of his paintings, my clear favorite is *Boy with a Red Vest*, which I used to be allowed to copy—with no questions asked—at Durand-Ruel's in Paris before it luckily came to this country. I could just walk in with my watercolors and sit there struggling with what I saw, trying to understand what made it so satisfactory. Even the texture of that oil paint, the sensitivity of Cézanne's touch on that specific linen, are proof enough of his genius. I have also greatly liked many of the *Mont Sainte-Victoire* oils and watercolors.

Of all paintings, my favorite without any question is Pierro della Francesca's *Resurrection* in Borgo San Sepolchro.

Of contemporary paintings, I would like most to own and enjoy Matisse's 1914 *Port Fenêtre à Collioure*, with its simple blue-grey, green, and black panels; and a very cool, light, and exquisite analytical cubist Picasso that the Goodspeed family in Chicago once owned, perhaps still do.

I am filled with such joy standing in Masaccio's Santa Maria del Carmine in Florence, or gazing at late Rembrandts, many Goyas, some Velásquez, early Corots, Monets, Bonnards, or looking at the whole splendid parade of Western artists—but the specific works I have named are the ones I love most.

My favorite sculpture is the Tang *Ram* from China, first seen only as a head in Roger Fry's *Transformations* back in 1923 and encountered, to my utter astonishment, as a complete animal at Asia House in New York City in 1980. The whole Tang period of Chinese culture seemed

Favorite Cézanne

able to abstract anything—be it a plant, an animal, or human being—and yet retain an inner vitality, mystery, and elegance.

Then Michelangelo's last work, the Virgin Mother holding the utterly dead and sagging son. In this tall, very thin piece with its extra arm, not yet chiseled away, she is at last looking *at* him. What aesthetic comprehension and sculptured passion! It is in Milan behind some very complicated areas in the Castello Sforza and should be seen.

During World War II, Picasso produced a boulder-like sculpted skull; mysterious, macabre, and indeed moving.

As to movies—the art form that I keenly feel is by far the most meaningful in our times—my two foremost preferences are Dovzhenko's *Earth* and Bresson's *Un Condamné à mort s'est échappé* (*A Condemned Man Escapes*). After those two masterpieces, many Keatons and many Chaplins.

Other favorites

ON DRAWING

By drawing a lot, and painting some, I have managed to record all that I have keenly felt since I was a small boy.

Relying on a mixture of feelings, intuition, objects, and the individuality of people, I have evoked my world. Not at first, but later and after considerable reading of Jung around 1935, I began to get at how things felt—not so much how things look as how they *feel*. The quest has provided endless hours of release and enjoyment.

How does the artist present areas of experience? What of the unconscious, which has now become as real and rich as those serene and manageable exteriors of Constable and Corot? The subjective sensations have become as credible as objective reality.

I slowly sensed that I could at least portray one aspect of human experience; that since childhood I had had an empathy for the flow of emotions. Starting with movement and motion, I had also keenly felt my joys and tastes, the fear of heights, the terrors of night, the dread of the attic steps alone when I turned the corner leading upward and the lights of the house below ended. How do we render aggressions, the nature of incompetence and sloth? Or draw how blindness feels at the back of failing eyes? How can one transpose into images fatigue, woe, what it means to be a conservative, how music and poetry feel? These questions have interested me endlessly.

People ask me how I think of myself—as an artist, a cartoonist, a social critic? I tend to reply "as a drawer," for my real pleasure has been in drawing. When color or texture or organization is needed I can fall back on that early training in the academies in Rome and Paris and I can use what I learned there. In the course of sixty years of drawing, a broad and flowing line evolved that suited me. I didn't try for it; it simply emerged out of *my* visual and interior needs.

I know that the subjects I choose to draw have been clearly influenced by the moral convictions that evolved as I grew up. As a boy I saw my father and mother seek justice when legal injustices were being committed and stand firmly against what they believed to be corrupt, deceitful, or plain chicanery. Later, as I became able to speak clearly with pictures, I also felt able to attack the many injustices which man seems to have an infinite capacity to create and sustain. It was heartening to learn from the mathematician John von Neumann that he felt that the drawings I did for *Strategy in Poker, Business and War* explained more than the text. I went on to attack the manifold international follies, including, of course, the BOMB—that final insanity, far beyond justice or injustice.

It was odd about Joe McCarthy, that shameless senator from Wisconsin. In his case my own emotions simply couldn't be brought under usable control. Otherwise, with luck, I have usually been able to set down my reactions to life around me, in short, the human predicament in this less than perfect world.

It is perhaps impossible to describe the tactile pleasures of drawing, finally, on superb unfoxing Arches paper with just the right texture for me. Too, there are English etching inks; German inks that do not change even when exposed to years of hot and blinding sun; Czechoslovakian leads that don't develop a bacterial "bloom" as American leads too often do; and Chinese brushes, easily obtained nowadays, which seem to do half of the work. It probably took six thousand years to create them. Foinet's incredibly beautiful array of pastel sticks are not only a pleasure to use, but just to contemplate—the range of subtle tones is a delight in itself. These are the quiet, untormented pleasures of the artist.

Of course, there is also the pleasure of drawing anything one wishes to draw at the moment: the cooling salmon somehow made to look silvery white on white paper; or one of Elodie's pale roses, subtle beyond belief, attempted and at least studied, even if, in the end, one fails.

So one pursues all these various expressions of thought and feeling, and doing it, I can assure you is, on the whole, pure joy—although there are agonies at times in the struggle.

AN OSBORN
PORTFOLIO

THERE I WAS DANCING IN THE FALL

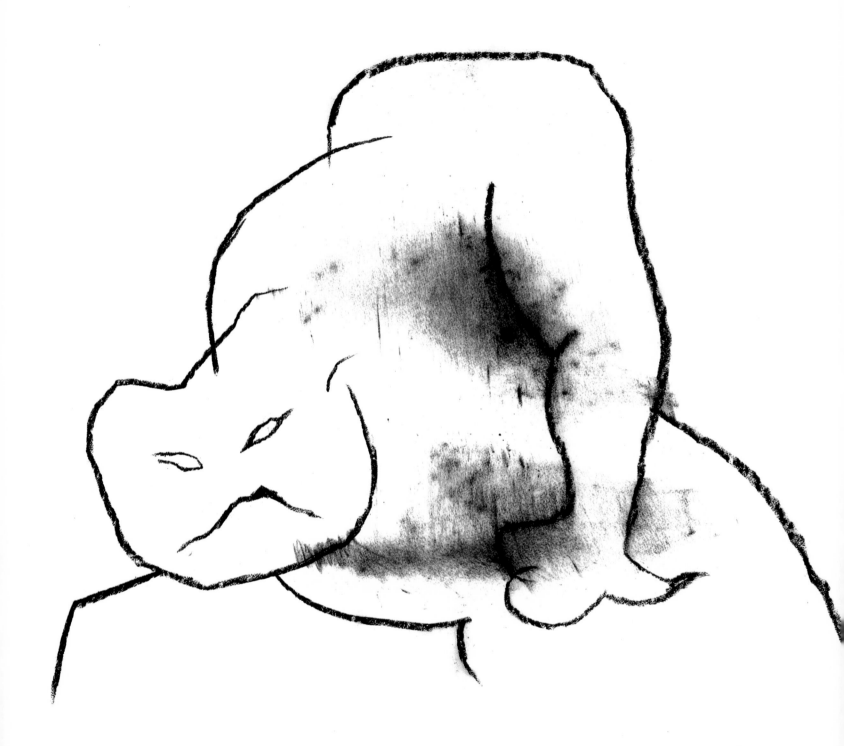

ANGER

98

FEAR

DEATH IS LOOKING AT *YOU*

THE HIT SOLDIER

100

AUSCHWITZ,   BUCHENWALD, DACHAU, BELSEN, TREBLINKA

KILL THE OTHERS

PROSECUTOR OF PETER REILLY

THE WAY I THINK OF SHAKESPEARE

GENE TUNNEY LECTURING   ON SHAKESPEARE AT YALE

FALSTAFF AS A PHEASANT

MENDELSSOHN'S MUSIC

HOMER'S WORDS

JOCKEY

110

RATTLESNAKE

MUSICIANS

114

ELIOT'S MONKEY, BUDDHA

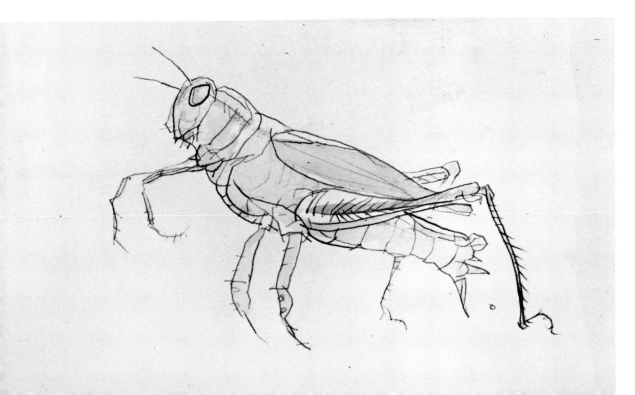

GRASSHOPPER

115

NOTRE DAME, PARIS

TACONIC RANGE

116

KEYSTONE KOPS

RUNNERS

120

CHAPLINS

JACQUES TATI

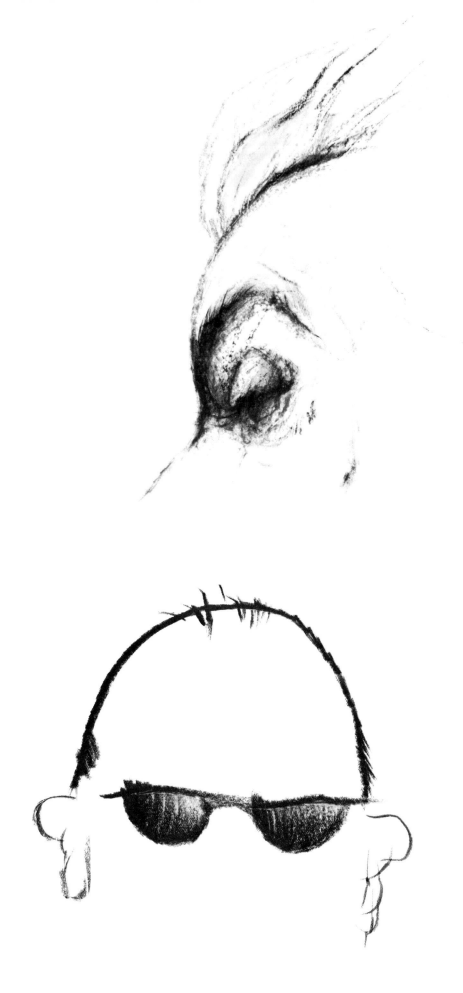

GARBO, ELVIS PRESLEY,
HOLLYWOOD PRODUCER

123

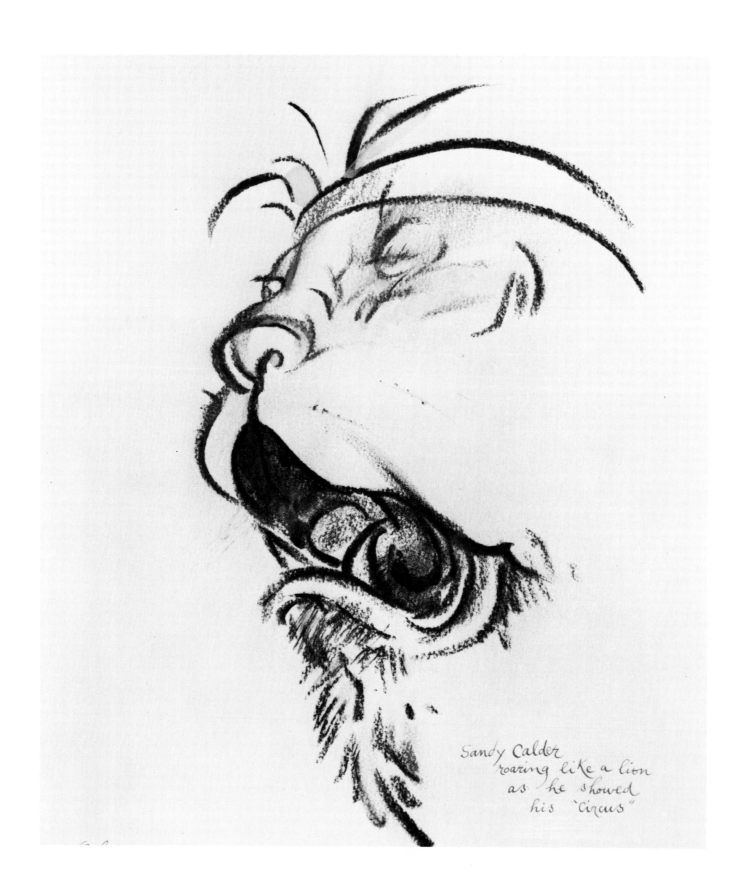

Sandy Calder
roaring like a lion
as he showed
his "Circus"

124

Calder

Osborn

Calders

Roxbury. Conn

Saché

FRA

Calder

Saché
I. et L.
France

CONNECTICUT NEIGHBOR

STRAVINSKY

MIRÓ

MAHLER'S MUSIC

THE LOWELLS

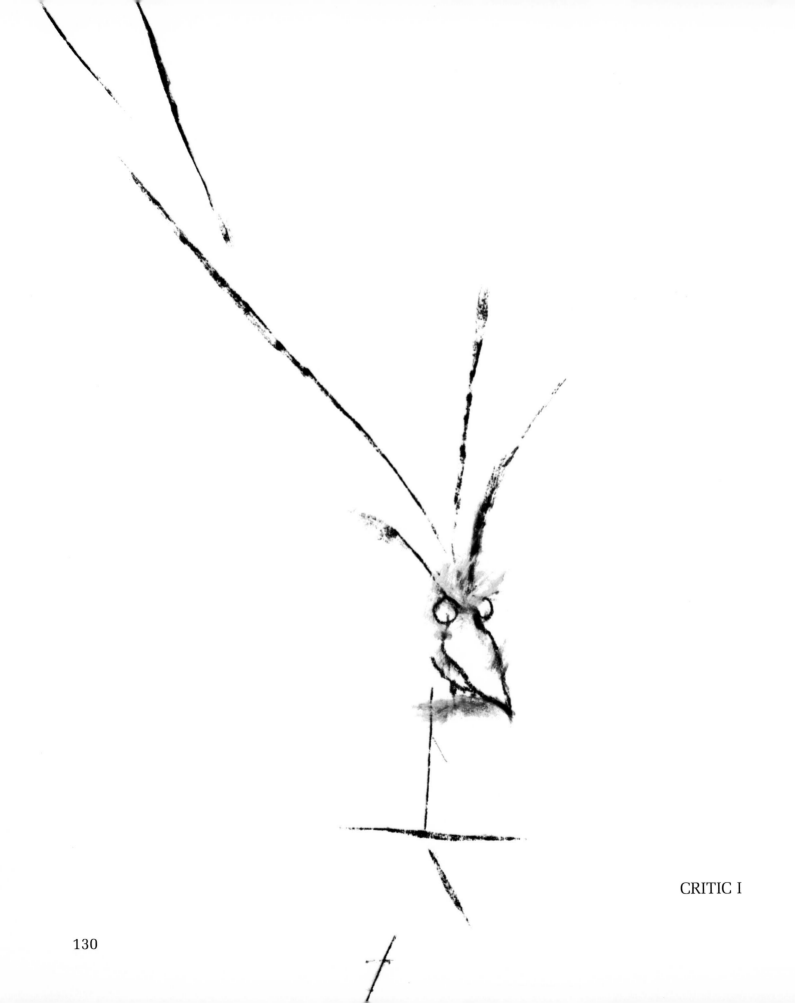

CRITIC I

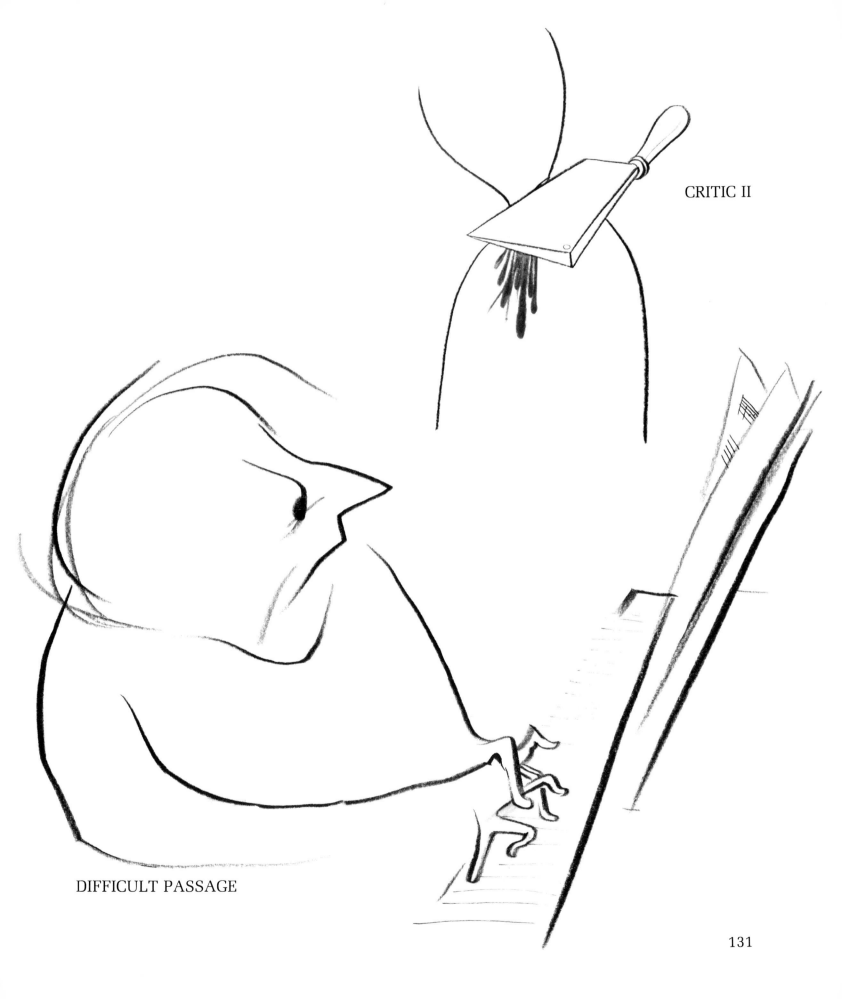

CRITIC II

DIFFICULT PASSAGE

131

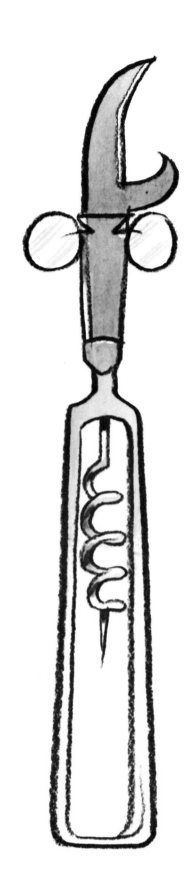

PSYCHIATRIST

WAR AND PEACE

PREMONITION

MORNING AFTER

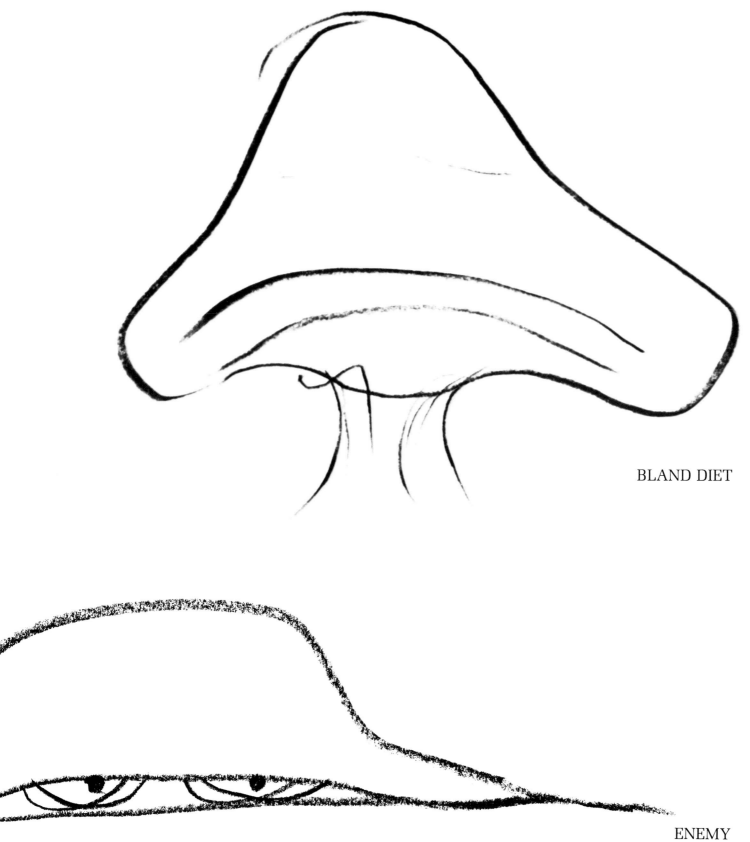

BLAND DIET

ENEMY

135

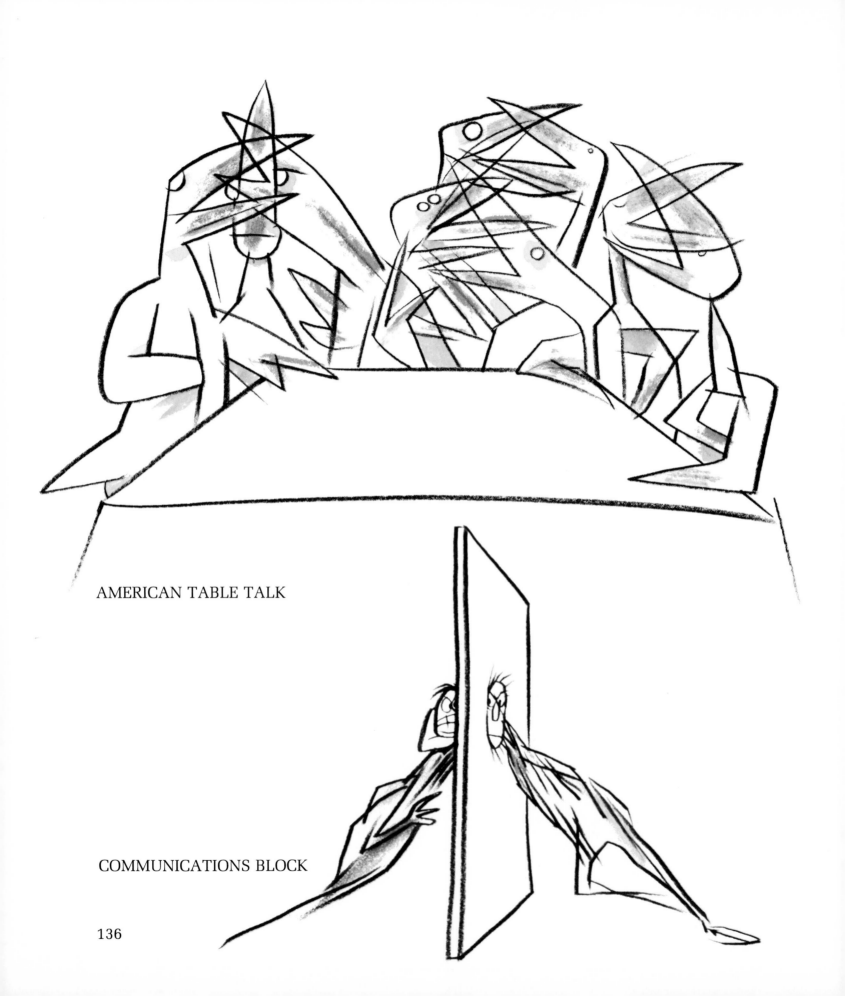

AMERICAN TABLE TALK

COMMUNICATIONS BLOCK

136

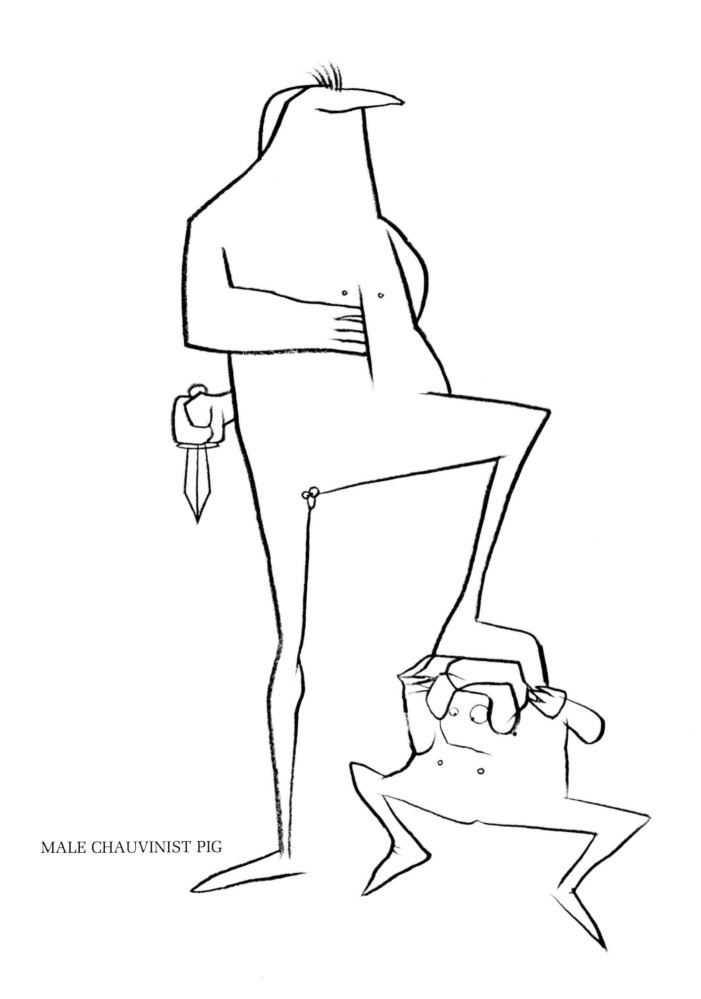

MALE CHAUVINIST PIG

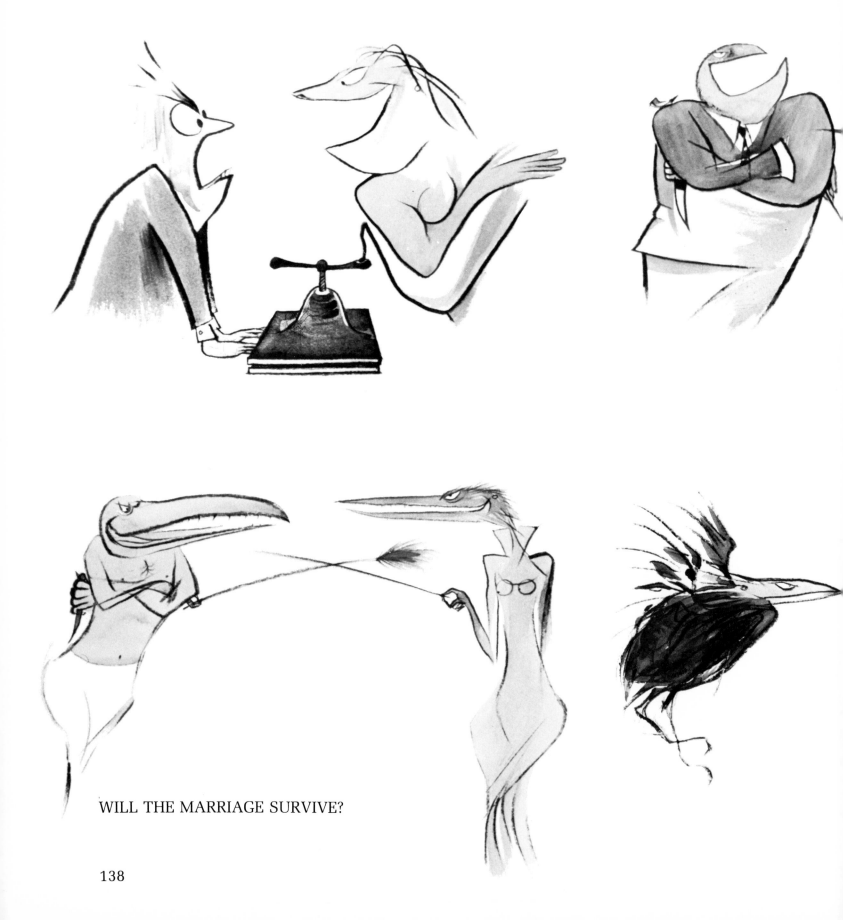

WILL THE MARRIAGE SURVIVE?

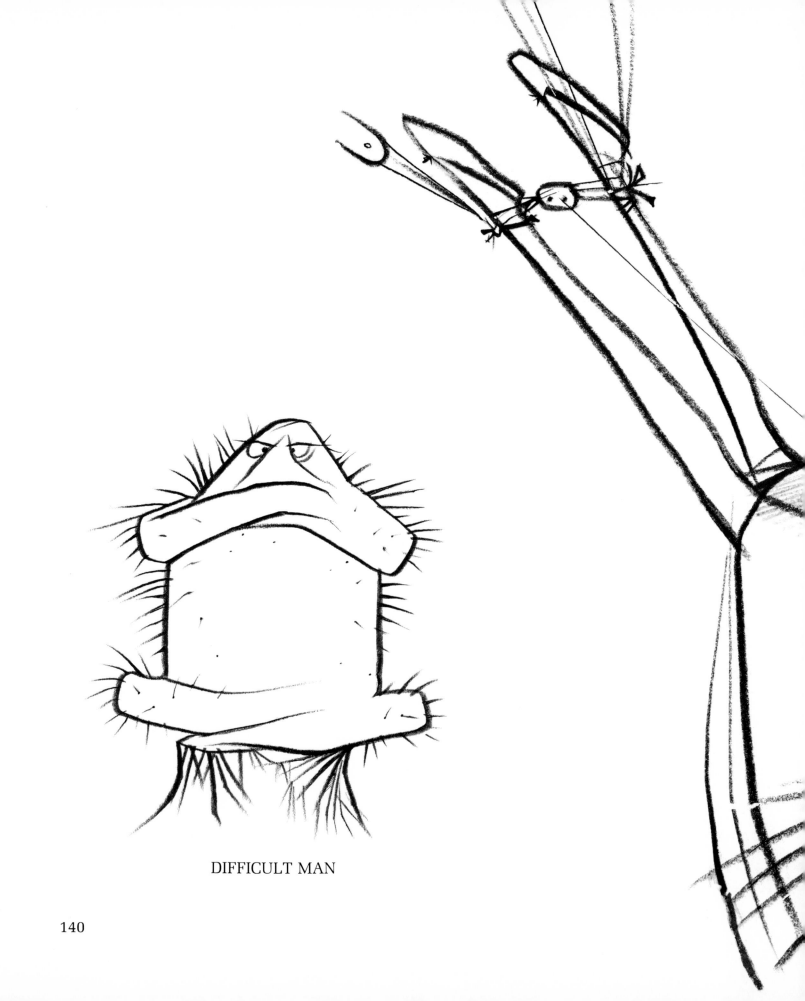

DIFFICULT MAN

A WOMAN'S DAY

RE

Robert Dylan

THE SIXTIES

BOB DYLAN

DETROIT

TOP EXEC

CAR STYLIST

THE CONSUMER
CULTURE

147

CHINA LOBBY

TV

DYNAMIC OBSOLESCENCE

149

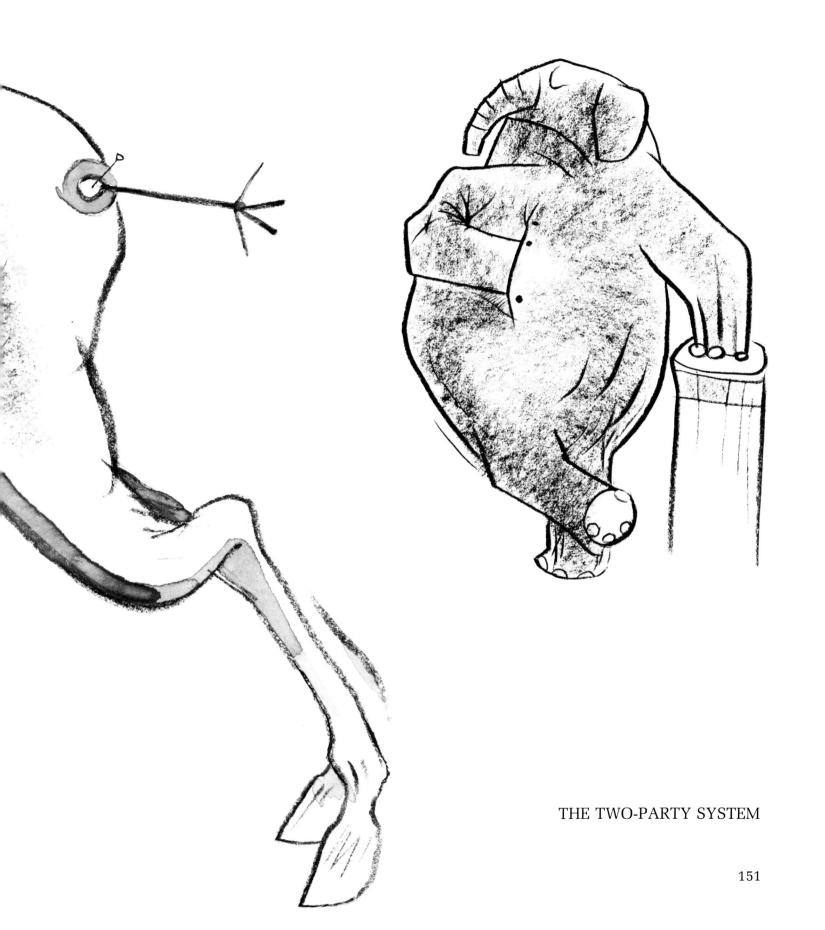

THE TWO-PARTY SYSTEM

NIXON

152

BRINKSMAN DULLES

154

TOP CLOWN, KHRUSHCHEV

GENERAL MAYHEM

THE GUN CULTURE

156

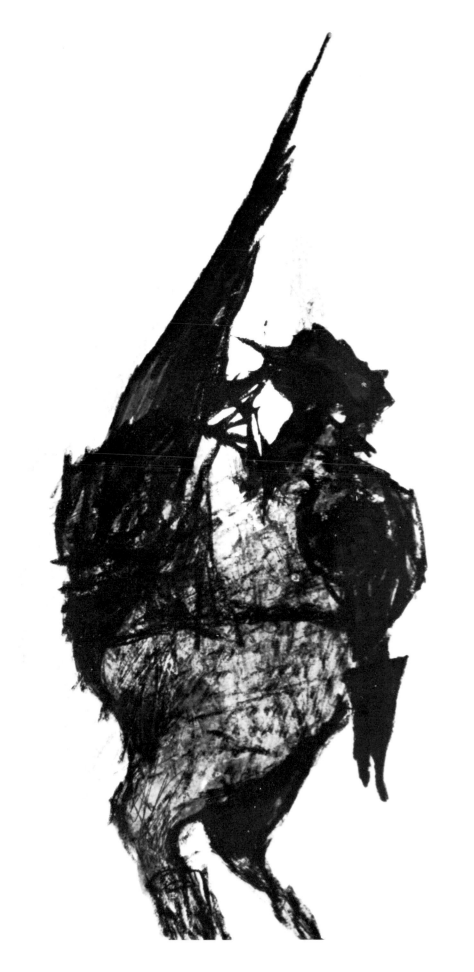

NAZI

157

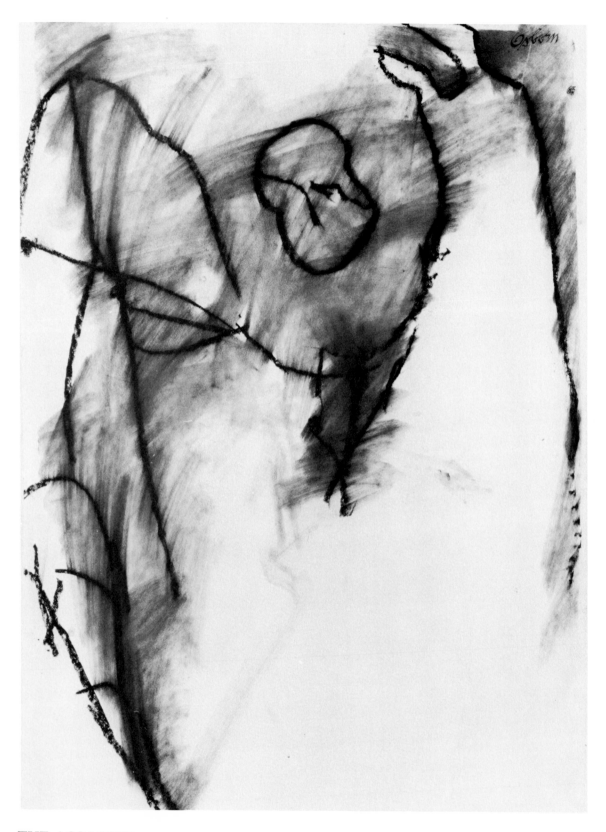

THE ASSASSIN

HOMAGE TO MEDGAR EVERS

Hom

1

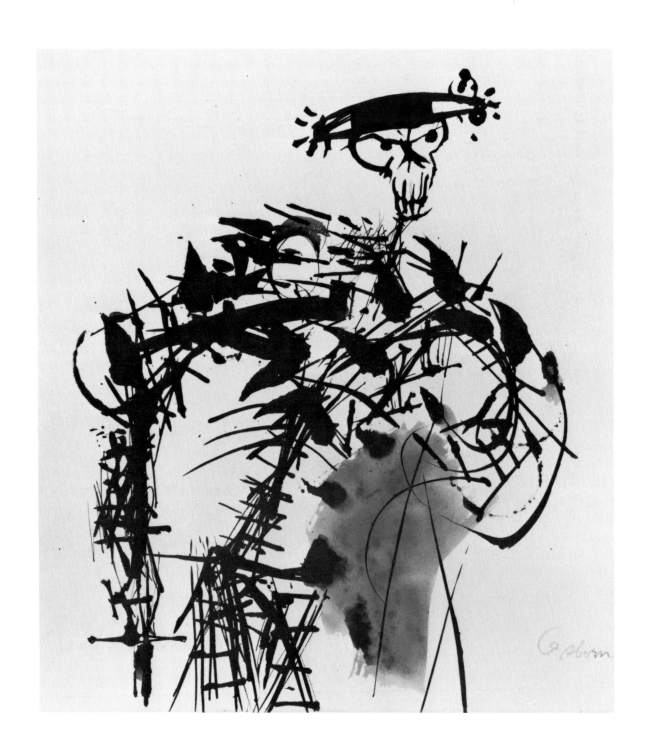

MATADORS

MORTAL COMBAT

MAN READY

VICTIM

MANKIND MAY NEVER MAKE IT

BRILLAT-SAVARIN, FRANCO

166

EINSTEIN

EDWARD ALBEE

SAMUEL BECKETT

Osborn

JAMES JOYCE

BUSTER KEATON

STUDIES FOR MURAL IN PORTUGAL

DETAIL FROM DAMAGED MURAL, SINCE DESTROYED

MODEL PLANE

BLÉRIOT

WRIGHT BROTHERS—KITTY HAWK

It works!

Westmore Cand

GENERAL WESTMORELAND

VIETNAM
WE BURN THEIR CHILDREN

their children
eyes & mouths
close!

Osborn

GRASSHOPPERS' LAST CONCERTO

STRONTIUM LOVES US ALL

BESIDE THE DANUBE

CASSIS-SUR-MER

TACONIC WINTER

CANVASBACK

MUSKRAT

SALMON

183

THE DAY CALDER DIED

LOVES/HATES

As I approach unfavoring death, I sense ever more acutely the things I loved and those things I hated, attacked, despised—call them what you will. To dispense at once with the loathsome: Mussolini was the first chest-thumping, bumptious fool to plague me, followed by his fat son, gleefully bombing the pitiful Ethiopians and writing poems about his bombs bursting like "rosebuds" far below. I used to see Mussolini emerge, like some pouter cuckoo, onto the silly, small, rug-draped balcony overlooking the jam-packed Piazza Venezia to harangue . . . with PONDEROUS pauses . . . the cheering populace. The year was 1929. All told, it was a dismal introduction to Italy and her people.

Then came the unspeakably warped and truly evil Hitler. And ghastly Stalin, in his paranoid terror, destroying the meaning and possible contributions of his remarkably creative nation—its music, literature, airplane design, theater, pure science, ballet, film. Nearly every cultural exploration was strangled in that sad land by that one cruel specimen from the provinces. Thousands of the perceptive elite were destroyed and what remains is a fenced-in compound run by small-eyed, suspicious peasants in city clothes . . . of sorts.

Or take, for hating, that whole poisonous Civil War in Spain. What truly incensed me was the fact that, although the Republican government had been legally elected by the majority, the selfish rich and the cloned military could not, and would not accept that outcome. So, mounting sufficient fire-power they regained (thanks to testing Hitler and strutting, waist-pinching "Musso"), what they had clearly lost at the ballot box. Spain has paid, over many years, a dear price for that chicanery and only now recovers from its torments, slowly.

Fortunately, my anger at all of this still happily exists within me and can be called forth almost too easily against those things that I dislike, distrust, or that bespeak blind folly.

I once told that wonderfully original American, James Thurber, that too many things were beginning to annoy or anger me. He fixed his single eye on me and shot back, "Why, I'm good and MAD by four o'clock *every* morning."

* * *

The two most distasteful, dismaying facts in my life are these: WITHIN MY LIFETIME MAN HAS KILLED 65 MILLION OF HIS OWN SPECIES. NO OTHER FORM SO VICIOUSLY DESTROYS ITSELF.

The other is obviously the BOMB and the creation of ever more lethal and exacting weapons with their increasingly precise delivery systems. Each half year our hydrogen bombs, their hydrogen bombs, become more sophisticated and deadly. They are now so unbelievably powerful and blazingly destructive in their explosive-implosive force and molten heat that citizens can no longer begin to comprehend what these bombs, unleashed, will do to once triumphant life.

It impoverishes all thought that man's brain—inflamed by fears, refueled by the id—can conceive, and expensively build these contraptions of endless death and drifting wastes, yet refuse to address itself in sufficient degree to solving the self-inflicted problems of overpopulation, water, energy, or our despoiling of the sky, the land, and thus the sea.

Snarling men of late exhibit the characteristics of crowded rats. Hardly a month now passes without a new configuration of clear or brooding hatred on some border, in some city, or even within political bodies—as though the id, like Caliban, has once again emerged to take control.

* * *

Then there is the other side of life, which I have been fortunate enough to enjoy during the many splendid years—the choice and varied moments, the exquisite pleasures. Spring and summer luncheons, well remembered. Indigo blue-black wind storms coming over the mountain's rim. Fresh green figs, quartered and bathed in cream. The early transparent plane wings, the linen stretched into dipping curves across the carved and sanded ribs, then carefully shellacked. All model planes and their small engines. Racing in fast inland sailboats or cruising in heavier ones along the eastern seaboard.

The various national foods, never too heavy, from Oshkosh to the small patron-run hotel in Balleroy, France. Elodie's superb cooking, tasted carefully by the mouthful.

The warmth and texture of the other sex, always revealing, always sensed after the slightest change. And the entire range and mystery of shared enjoyment—well beyond the porno fantasies now sold the young from lower drugstore shelves.

Elodie reading aloud something we both want to hear. She reads with a fine lyric sense of words and without affectations of speech.

We derive great pleasure from listening to music, and going to movies we want to see together. And looking at any work of art. All Pieros, seen together, in those well-distributed galleries in Italy. Many Cézannes; a small, dark, grey-green Guardi one can hardly tear oneself away from in Milan's Museo Poldi Pozzoli. Vermeer! The mosaics at Torcello or Ravenna. Specific works that we have enjoyed together would be endless. And buildings. . . . Le Corbusier's La Tourette outside of Lyon, now in serious disarray; or the enormous dignity of Notre Dame, still intact despite the stone wounds from German fire that mar her *place*; the Pazzi Chapel in Florence; finally, Chartres, her disparate spires strangely moving on every encounter. And the translucent Matisse chapel at Vence, so carefully wrought and satisfactory in every interior detail, even when packed with Japanese tourists clad in cameras, chattering like small animals, totally oblivious to the aged Mother Superior screaming "Silence!" in Marseillaise French.

*   *   *

To add one musician to all of these riches, great and small, I suggest that Mozart (who happens to please me even more than Beethoven at his best) certainly stands as one of the four or five true geniuses in Western culture. Relentlessly pursued and tormented by crushing problems, any one of which would wither our interiors, he nevertheless poured forth music of such exquisite invention, beauty, and proper meaning that it is difficult to believe. Or that, in fact, syphilis killed him when he was but thirty-two. And society's reward was a pauper's grave.

I won't go into troubled Michelangelo, beset Rembrandt, or Leonardo, that giant, banished from his homeland to die in France. Yet their immense talents afford all of us the most intense pleasure. By comparison, well-treated bankers, insurance grinders, conglomerate gluers, and plumbers look like computerized harpooners.

* * *

Edward Larrabee Barnes was the architect of our house. He was fresh out of Harvard, and had been taught well by Gropius and Breuer. The house is modest, and, as Isabel Wilder observed, both formal and informal. It has been a pleasure to live in with its ever varying light, serene proportions and careful, clear details. Dan Kiley's formal bosquet has been no detriment!

Marcel Breuer is another architect I have always enjoyed. He was by far the most articulate and lucid man I have known; Robert Motherwell, a close and very civilized second.

* * *

One of the gentle rewards of living in the country has been the wildlife which surrounds us at the least expected moments. There are the ever increasing numbers of Canadian geese, filling the valley with their odd, self-revealing cacophony each spring and fall. And far above them golden eagles hunt in pairs; they are immense on the wing, and rare, but there. Close at hand: all manner of birds, some passing in their flights north and south but more than enough living all about us; their "territory" songs often joyful, their plumage occasionally gemlike. The infinite wild flowers and butterflies are free gifts.

Deer used to be scarce in our part of Connecticut. Encountering one in the woods was always a delicate experience, unless an antlered buck, in rut, turned on you, horns lowered like a Spanish bull, and you had to keep a tree trunk between the two of you until he, disgusted, departed . . . snorting.

Now deer of all ages are becoming a trial for farmers, fruitgrowers, and gardeners. On early spring mornings we've seen as many as forty deer feeding on the crest of our hill, looking like one of those dawn shots taken of

House and Studio

vast African herds. Without too much guilt I now apply each year for state permission to kill one deer. Our garden gains, and a properly cured, properly broiled rack of venison is something even the best Parisian restaurant cannot provide; just as an American ruffed grouse with *al dente* wild rice cannot be equaled—particularly when it travels but ten feet from the hot Aga stove to your place at the table, with no underpaid, lackluster, loitering waiter delaying its arrival.

Finally, and perhaps most wonderful of all, are those things we tend to take for granted—the way genes behave, for one. I marvel endlessly at the correct placement of each tiny leg on even the most minuscule of insects; at the rhythmic order of life that has kept the mallard ducks we see today looking exactly like the ones that march by us in ancient Egyptian murals; in short, at the whole scheme of things, repeating or evolving under their own forces upon this earth.